TO WIN AT BRIDGE

Have You Got What It Takes?

Ron Klinger

Weidenfeld & Nicolson
IN ASSOCIATION WITH
PETER CRAWLEY

First published in Great Britain 2007
in association with Peter Crawley
by Weidenfeld & Nicolson
a division of the Orion Publishing Group Ltd
Orion House, 5 Upper St Martin's Lane, London WC2H 9EA

10 9 8 7 6 5 4 3 2 1

A catalogue record for this book
is available from the British Library

ISBN 978 0 297 85351 0

Typeset by Modern Bridge Publications
P.O. Box 140, Northbridge NSW 1560, Australia

Printed in Great Britain by
Clays Ltd, St Ives plc

The Orion Publishing Group's policy is to use papers that
are natural, renewable and recyclable products and made
from wood grown in sustainable forests. The logging and
manufacturing processes are expected to conform to the
environmental regulations of the country of origin.

www.orionbooks.co.uk

TO WIN AT BRIDGE
Have You Got What It Takes?

Winners are grinners, losers chagriners. Winning may not be everything, but it certainly beats the feeling you have when you come second. Some even say, 'Winning isn't everything, it's the only thing.' We all know that they don't engrave the names of the also-rans on trophies.

Why do we play bridge? Certainly it is an excellent pastime, a stimulating challenge, but the bottom line is that we all like to win, whether it is a social game, a local club pairs or an international tournament. There are always many competitors, but in the end it boils down to one winner, and you want that winner to be you.

In this book Australian expert Ron Klinger shows you how to be on the victory dais more often. There is heaps of advice on all aspects of the winning strategy, from the preparation you need to do before an event starts to how to cope with problems during a tournament and how to handle difficult partners.

In addition there are fifty problems to test your capabilities in bidding, opening leads, defence and declarer play. Even if you do not perform well on these at first, your game will improve significantly if you absorb the principles in the solutions to the problems.

Ron Klinger is a leading international bridge teacher and has represented Australia in many world championships since 1976. He has written over fifty books, some of which have been translated into Bulgarian, Chinese, Danish, French, Hebrew and Icelandic.

Contents

Introduction

Do you simply turn up at a tournament a few minutes early and sit down at your table ready to start playing? Do you realise that there is much you can do beforehand to improve your winning chances? Do you ever warm up before a session? What about looking after yourself and your partner during a session?

There is more to winning than simply being a strong player. That must help, of course, but you can increase your winning percentage by improving yourself and your partnership in many ways other than merely bridge knowledge and technique. This book offers many tips to give you and your partnership a winning edge, to help you to victory more often.

The first two chapters cover ways to improve yourself and also your partnership. Chapter 3 contains lots of material on methods you might wish to implement in order to have a superior approach to bidding. If you are not ready for that yet, by all means skip Chapter 3. Leave it for the time being and come back to it later when you and your partner are keen to enhance your system.

The second half of the book contains quizzes on bidding, leads, defence and declarer play. Make sure you give each problem plenty of thought before flicking to the solution. There is good news. Most of the top-level players who faced these problems originally did not find the right answer at the table. You can do better and if you come with the right answer to more than 50 per cent of the problems, you do have what it takes to win at bridge.

Happy bridging.

Ron Klinger, 2007

Chapter 1

You

The single most important factor in the equation for winning is *you*. Of course, there are many other factors, your partner, the opponents, even luck, but the only one over which you have control is yourself. Since you want to win, you owe it to yourself to make sure you are in the best possible condition for winning. This refers not just to your mental state, but a good physical condition is also a benefit.

That is not to say you require the fitness of an Olympic athlete, but you do need the fitness to last through a session or many sessions if the tournament is a long one. It is said that one session of bridge takes more energy, more stamina and imposes greater stress than a brain surgeon conducting a 3-hour operation. Where the brain surgeon is dealing with one problem, albeit a very complex one, bridge players deal with twenty to thirty problems, each lasting 6-7 minutes. No wonder you can tire easily towards the end of a session.

Tournaments can last a weekend, and a week or a fortnight is common for major national and international events, with two or three sessions a day. It is no surprise that those who are not used to the strain of so many consecutive sessions start to wilt in the middle of a long tournament. Standard of play drops dramatically as fatigue takes over and the mind can no longer cope. What we could do easily when fresh is now a great burden. The longer we continue the greater the mental overload and we make mistakes which are totally embarrassing. Obviously this is something we want to avoid.

What can you do easily to improve your fitness and stamina? *Clearly you must not adopt any of the following suggestions without consulting your doctor, so please make sure you have done that before proceeding.*

It will repay you greatly to include 30-45 minutes exercise daily. The degree of exercise will depend on your age and physical condition, but it does not need to be too strenuous. Walking and/or swimming are ideal. Choose a pace that suits you, but do not make it leisurely. It should be a brisk walk, not a stroll. If you are mildly out of breath and perspiring at the end of the exercise, that is just about right.

How brisk is brisk? Again this will vary from person to person, but I find that 110-120 steps per minute is brisk for me. You will need to fix your own yardstick.

If you are overweight, as many of us are, then ask your doctor to recommend a dietician to create a program for you to drop the excess gradually and safely. The less weight you carry, the easier it becomes to last through a long event. A combination of regular exercise and a healthy diet is the best way to reduce your weight.

Alcohol

More will be said about that in Chapter 5 when you are at a tournament, but a moderate intake of alcohol is fine on your non-bridge days. Here, too, individuals differ greatly so you need to be the judge of how much alcohol is 'moderate'. Since a glass of red wine daily is recommended as an anti-oxidant, that is a reasonable yardstick. Again, it is best to adhere to your doctor's recommendation.

Smoking

Don't.

The evidence is very strong that smoking can curtail your life. If you want to play bridge for as long as possible (and don't we all want to do that?), then it makes no sense to retain a habit which is likely to cut down your lifespan. Smoking also increases the risk of various illnesses, many of which are unpleasant and can be long-lasting. If you do fall ill, that will cut down your opportunities for bridge, not to mention the distress of the illness itself. When you do become ill, you might be letting down your bridge partner and perhaps your team-mates, too. You might also miss out on events in which you wanted to take part.

Many bridge clubs are now non-smoking. So are many major tournaments, both national and international. If you are a smoker at these events, it simply adds to your stress when you are desperate for a smoke. There is enough stress during a bridge session. You do not need any extra. Some events do provide some breaks, so that can be of some help.

It is easy to say, 'Give up smoking', but very difficult to do. There are many programs which can help you to stop. I urge you to do so. If you manage to stop, you will feel much better for it, as will your bridge partners.

If you are a non-smoker and play at a club or in a tournament where smoking is permitted, you would be better off not to take part. Passive smoking is also a health risk. Play at a non-smoking club. Limit your games to non-smoking events. If this is not possible, then try to step outside the smoke-filled area into fresh air as often as possible.

Drugs. Don't do drugs. No more need be said. If you do take drugs and play bridge, stop well before any serious tournament if you want to play at your best. If not for yourself, you owe it to your partner or team-mates.

Caffeine. Coffee and bridge-playing seem to go hand in hand, but it is not essential. Those who have given up coffee and other caffeine products have reported no detrimental effect in regard to their bridge ability. Some have suggested that they are playing better.

The mental side

You need to be a tough competitor, not physically aggressive but mentally tough. You cannot let outside elements affect you or your concentration, whether it is noise or comments by partner or by the opponents. You can choose to be angry or choose not to be angry. You can choose to be embarrassed or choose not to. Choosing 'not to' works much better. With practice and without undue effort, you can control your emotions so that they do not affect your bridge or any other part of your life. Simply let any criticism flow over you and pay it no heed during a game.

Another important aspect is to avoid negative thoughts and avoid phrasing your aims in negative form. Think 'We are going to win this match' rather than 'We are not going to lose this match' and 'We will defeat them' instead of 'They will not beat us'.

Set your aims high. It is amazing, and disappointing, to hear teams say, "We will be happy to reach the quarter-finals." They should be saying, "We will win the championship."

Believe low and you will achieve low. Your mind is amazing and has untapped reserves. A positive approach can produce incredible results. Do not be satisfied with second place. Aim for the sky.

Memory and concentration

You do not need to be a great mathematician to play bridge well. Yes, some arithmetic is needed, but a much greater factor is logic. In addition, memory and concentration play a huge role. These topics are too great to cover in a single chapter and more will be said later. For more information on these areas, see *Improve Your Bridge Memory* for short term memory and *Better Bridge with a Better Memory* to improve your long term memory.

Improving your present standard

There are several ways that can help you to become a better all-round player. One is to study books. Generally, books on card play are more helpful than those on bidding. If you are relatively new to bridge, then *Guide To Better Card Play, Guide To Better Duplicate, 100 Winning Bridge Tips* and *100 Winning Duplicate Bridge Tips* are all useful. For the strong player headed for expert level, you will already have read, or make sure you do read *Card Play Technique* (Mollo & Gardner), any card play book by Victor Mollo or by Hugh Kelsey (especially *Killing Defence at Bridge*) or by Eddie Kantar. Do not miss *How To Read Your Opponents' Cards* (Mike Lawrence), *Dormer on Deduction* (Albert Dormer), *Reese on Play* and *The Expert Game* (Terence Reese) or *Card Reading* (Eric Jannersten). Any book with card play quizzes and problems is worth a look.

The expert will already be familiar with these great works: *Bridge with the Blue Team* (Pietro Forquet), *Adventures in Card Play* (Geza Ottlik and Hugh Kelsey), as well as the annual world championship books. For the average player, these are all quite difficult, so be prepared.

Most countries have a monthly or bi-monthly magazine. You should take out a subscription. Many newspapers carry a daily or weekly bridge column, which can be instructive.

There are now CDs and DVDs for bridge. The big plus is that they are interactive and you can play and replay the deals. You will not go wrong if you acquire any on card play by Larry Cohen or Mike Lawrence.

In times past a strong recommendation was to visit a club to watch the top players in action. Almost none object to your watching (as long as you are quiet) and are happy to answer polite questions. That advice is still good today, but now it is much easier to watch the top players without leaving home. There are many internet bridge websites where you can play or learn, read articles or watch the experts play each other. One of the best of these sites is Bridge Base Online (BBO). You can download the software from www.bridgebase.com and you are ready to go. Not only can you play in their tournaments, use the material in their library, but you can also organise private matches or practise bidding with your partner.

On most days of the year there are live matches from the major tournaments around the world. You can see the bidding, follow the play and there are experts giving commentary as the play unfolds. The best news is that, at the time of writing, BBO is free.

Chapter 2

Your partner

What qualities should you seek when looking for a bridge partner? The most important quality is ambition. You and your partner should be equally ambitious. If you want to represent your country internationally, it is futile for that purpose to play with someone who just wants to play club bridge once a week. Most of us have several partners, some for casual games, others for serious endeavours.

As with marriage, partners are not perfect. You must be able to accept them, warts and all. If their faults are too much to bear, do not persevere. You are intent on winning, but the bridge itself must be a pleasant experience.

Some partners are constantly critical. Get rid of them. Some partners are *never* wrong. If you obtain a bad score, it is always *your* fault. Get rid of them.

It helps greatly if you and partner are good friends. You need to be able to discuss your bad results constructively after the session without partner taking offence. Where friendship exists, there is no problem. In other cases you need to tread carefully.

Time and work also come into consideration. If you want to play three times a week and partner can play only once a fortnight, you have a problem. If you want to attend events overseas, but partner cannot get time off work, you have a conflict. It is better to sort out such differences before you start playing together.

A partner with a sense of humour is to be cherished. If you and partner can accept losses philosophically and even laugh them off, the partnership will be all the stronger for it. If that is not possible, you will need to resolve your differences in a way that suits both of you. Talking calmly, courteously and respectfully is essential.

If possible, play with someone who is better than you. Your partner can then help you to improve and they will certainly want you to do that. In such a partnership, do not be afraid to ask for partner's advice. That will be helpful for you and also flattering for partner.

If thinking of playing with someone of approximately equal standard, you should have respect for the quality of their game. If you do not have that, then there will be friction and that is something that must be avoided.

If you are clearly the stronger partner, you have already made up your mind to accept partner's shortfalls. When pointing out how partner might have done better, always do it softly and kindly.

Should husbands and wives play together? The advantage is that you can easily practice your bidding and discuss your methods and results. Nevertheless it takes considerable effort to make such a partnership work if winning is your aim. At top level there are very few such successful partnerships. Emotion can cloud your judgment and the kindest of spouses can sometimes say the unkindest words. For social games, by all means play with your spouse. If you aim at county, national or international success, be warned that it is tougher to play with a spouse than a partner you do not see daily.

There are countless stories about the pitfalls of playing with your spouse. At one of my classes in England, a lady told me how she made sure that her husband always treated her with great courtesy. "Before we go out to play," she said, "I turn down the bed in the spare room. He knows what awaits him if he does not behave."

Should you choose a partner of the same sex or doesn't it matter? In theory it should not make any difference and there are plenty of very strong mixed partnerships. It has nothing to do with ability. Men and women can play equally well.

Problems can arise for a mixed partnership when one or both partners are married. A non-bridge playing spouse might already resent your playing bridge instead of spending time with them. Playing with someone of the opposite sex can exacerbate the situation. Even if unwarranted, jealousy can rear its head.

It is best if both spouses play at the same venue at the same time. A good idea is to sit at the same compass point as your spouse. Then you can discuss the deals when you come home and compare your decisions.

Even if both spouses play bridge, problems can arise. If you are at top level, will your spouse be able to accept your playing overseas with a partner of the opposite sex? It is easier to avoid such conflict when choosing a bridge partner.

Is it better to have one partner or several? The advantage of just one partner is that you have just one set of methods. With several partners you might have various different systems to learn and remember. The downside of one partner is that they might become ill when a major event is on.

One of the early items on your agenda with a new partner is agreeing on your system. Some players have pet conventions which they insist on including. You might even have some yourself. Some compromise will usually be necessary.

At your first discussion about system you will deal with the broad sweep of system. As soon as possible you need to complete the many details so that misunderstandings will not be frequent. Make sure that you cover your slam methods, what to do when there is interference in your auctions, your defensive methods including doubles, overcalls, bids of the opposition suit, as well as your card play agreements.

It is sensible to have system notes, which need to be updated whenever you and partner add or change an agreement. You must know your system thoroughly. Read and re-read the notes until there is no unfamiliar area. One idea is to create flash cards for yourself (quiz on one side, answers on the other) so that you can test yourself and refresh your memory frequently. Another is for partners to give each other regular quizzes on system areas. It is silly to have a bad score because you forgot part of your system.

Some pairs agree that each system memory lapse in competition incurs a fine. The fine kitty will swell until you can convert it into lottery tickets or a dinner or something similar.

After each session it is important for both partners to go through the results. Do not worry about the good boards – mostly you are doing the right thing here already. Focus on the bad ones. Do not concern yourselves with whose fault it was. Discuss dispassionately how the result could have been improved. The aim is to fix the mistake, not the blame.

How often should you play in tournaments? As often as possible. If you are playing only once a week, you will want to practise at least once or twice a week as well. You can do this by playing against another pair, either at home or more easily on the internet, or by having bidding practice sessions. One of the best websites for either playing or partnership bidding is Bridge Base Online (see page 14). You will also find bidding quizzes in most bridge magazines.

If you want to practise slam bidding without using the 'net, a good approach is take a pack of cards and remove twenty random low cards (from the ten down). Deal two hands of thirteen cards each from the remaining pack of 32 cards. Leave the six remaining cards face down. Bid the two hands without any opposition bidding. You will find that the hands warrant a game, a small slam or a grand slam. Write the auction down so that you can discuss it later and iron out any misunderstandings if you have not found the best contract. As slam deals occur relatively rarely, a session of thirty such practice hands is equivalent to about thirty sessions of play in terms of slams.

If you have a supportive spouse or friend, they can set up some boards for you both to play against another equally keen pair (possibly your team-mates). Choosing deals from a major tournament, preferably a world championship, works well. The deals are played and when completed each player receives a photocopy of the deal, the bidding and play, together possibly with expert commentary. You can then compare your performance with that of the players in that international event. It will encourage you to see that they are not always perfect either, whether in the bidding or in the play.

Chapter 3

Your methods

Your methods, including your philosophy to the game, will also be critical when you are choosing a partner. Some like to be freewheelers, with mostly natural bidding and as few conventions as possible. Others are 'scientists', who want the greatest possible accuracy in the bidding. They tend to be perfectionists, as far as that is possible in the bidding. Some scientists like to play many conventions, others like to use 'relay bidding' when they hold strong hands.

Natural bidding is primarily dialogue, with each partner describing their hand. Relay bidding is question-and-answer with one partner in control, constantly asking the other, who describes the hand fully. The relayer normally makes the final decision and gives away little information in the bidding aside from holding a strong hand.

It does not work well for a scientist to partner a freewheeler. The latter either cannot learn the conventions or the relays or has little interest in doing so. What follows are frequent errors, which will be frustrating to you both and which will, of course, lead to poor scores. Freewheelers should play with other natural bidders, scientists should play with scientists.

It will not matter greatly whether your partnership consists of natural bidders or scientists. Both approaches have their losses and their triumphs. What is important is that you recognise into which group you fall (there are degrees in both camps) and you are both happy to follow your chosen approach.

If you are a relay pair, you already know your system. For natural bidders, you can quite happily follow your current methods or you might want to change to the approaches adopted by the leading players today. Each year a world championship book is published and reveals the methods used by the world's top players. This is a very good guide to what they judge to be most successful. Unless you are firmly wedded to your present bidding structure, you ought to consider what the experts are doing and perhaps amend your system accordingly.

One thing is for sure. There is no one superior system. How do we know that? Because if there was, everyone would be playing that system. At the world championships, there are dozens of different approaches. Some play four-card suits, others play 5-card majors. Some play a weak 1NT, others choose a mini-1NT (10-12) and some prefer a strong 1NT. Some play natural one-openings, others play an artificial, strong 1♣ opening. If any one of these could be proven to be better than the others, would not all the top players use that? Can you imagine any pair in a world contest adopting an approach which they feel is inferior to the ones played by other competitors?

The system you currently play tends to be the result of several factors: what your friends play, what is taught by the local teachers, what is the predominant method in your club and what is played by the top players in your area. The good news is that you are not obliged to stick with the methods that you have been using. You will not be ostracised if you decide to play something a little different from what is the mainstream local or even national approach. You and your partner should choose what works for you and what you believe is best.

Some questions are asked frequently.

Should we play 5-card majors or 4-card suits?
Both work and you should be able to play both methods. The main distinctions are the choice of opening bid and the greater frequency of a 3-card raise for a known 5-card major opening. In an uncontested auction you should reach the best contract whichever style you play. If an opening bid of 1♡ or 1♠ is followed by a jump-overcall, responder does have an easier time supporting opener if the major suit is known to be at least five. That might account for the slight majority of world class players in favour of 5-card majors.

Is it better to play a weak 1NT or a strong 1NT opening?
It really does not matter. Here, too, the devotees of each have their wins and losses. The 15-17 1NT allows the opponents into the auction cheaply when the opening is 1♣ or 1♢ with a minimum balanced hand. The 12-14 1NT will often play in 1NT and miss a better part-score when responder also has a balanced hand, but is not strong enough to respond. A big plus for the weak 1NT is responder's knowledge that when opener starts with a one-bid in a suit, the hand will be 15+ balanced or a shapely hand.

If the 2NT opening is played as 20-22, then using a 15-17 opening means that if opener is balanced and opens with a one-level suit bid, it will either be minimum (12-14) or very strong (18-19). This disparity makes it easier to compete later with the strong, balanced variety. Playing a weak 1NT, when a balanced opener starts with a suit bid of one, the range will be 15-19. This can prove difficult in competition when opener with 15-17 points feels the need to bid again. Take a look at this deal from a 2007 national teams event:

Dealer North : Love all

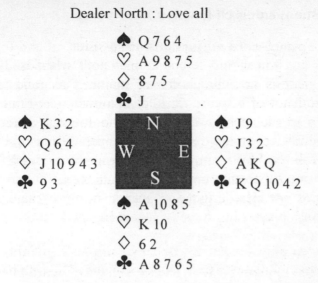

At one table East opened a strong 1NT, passed to North who bid 2♣, both majors. South chose 2♠, passed out and making nine tricks for +140.

At the other table East-West were playing a 12-14 1NT and the bidding went:

West	North	East	South
	No	1♣	1♠
1NT	3♠ (1)	Dble	All pass

(1) Pre-emptive raise

East felt obliged to take action with his 16-count and West saw no reason to push to the four-level. West led the ♣9. South won and played ♡K, heart to the ace, heart ruff with the ♠10. Next came the ♠5. West ducked and the ♠Q won. On the ♡8 from dummy, East ruffed with the ♠J and South discarded a diamond. East cashed a diamond, but South ruffed the next diamond, cashed the ♠A and had nine tricks, +530.

What about opening 1NT with a 5-card major?

The 2NT opening with a 5-card major has been around for a long time, but it used to be taboo to open 1NT when holding a 5-3-3-2 pattern including a 5-card major. The pendulum has swung the other way. At world championship level when an option arises to open 1NT or 1♡ or 1♠, the vast majority opt for the 1NT opening. There are a number of reasons for this. It gives less information to the opponents, especially if no major suit fit exists, and can thus attract a favourable lead. It does not impede game or slam bidding. It can keep the bidding lower and it removes some awkward rebid problems for a natural system.

If you decide to permit a 1NT opener to have a 5-card major, you will want responder to be able to discover that fact when responder has enough to try for game or slam and has some interest in a major suit fit. There is an easy approach by replacing simple Stayman with 5-card major Stayman.

1NT : 2♣ asks, 'Do you have a 5-card major?' Opener bids a major with five and 2♢ with no 5-card major. After 2♢, responder with game values can rebid 3♣ to ask, 'Do you have a 4-card major?' Opener replies accordingly.

Of course, there is much more available after the 1NT : 2♣ inquiry. If you and partner wish to take this further, you will find lots of information in *5-Card Major Stayman*, published by Cassell.

One advantage of locating a 5-card major in a balanced hand is that you can judge the right contract more easily. Would your partnership find the best spot on these cards:

```
WEST              EAST
♠  K 5            ♠  A 8 6
♡  A Q 9 6 4      ♡  K 7 5 3
♢  8 7 5          ♢  A 4 3
♣  A 4 2          ♣  9 8 6
```

If the bidding starts 1♡ : 3♡, would opener bid 3NT? Few would choose that. If opener bids 4♡, that will be one down. If opener passes 3♡ that will usually succeed, but the best spot of 3NT is missed.

As a 4-3-3-3 pattern opposite a 5-3-3-2 will often make the same number of tricks in no-trumps as in a trump contract, it will be important to be in 3NT when that number is nine. With 5-card major Stayman, the bidding can find the best spot: 1NT : 2♣, 3♡ : 3NT. The 3♡ reply can be used to show five hearts and a maximum 1NT (playing 12-14).

Some modern developments and new ideas

1. Bypassing a major with the 1NT rebid

You open 1♣ with a balanced hand including four spades and four clubs. After partner responds 1♢ or 1♡, should you rebid 1♠ or 1NT with the appropriate strength? The modern style is to rebid 1NT and bypass the major. There is a mild risk of missing a 2-level major suit part-score, but there are significant compensating advantages.

Partner will know your hand is not balanced when the bidding starts 1♣ : 1♢, 1♠ or 1♣ : 1♡, 1♠. For these sequences opener is known to have 4+ spades and 5+ clubs. If 4-4-1-4 rebid 1♡, and for 4-1-4-4 open 1♢.

If the bidding has started 1♣ : 1◇, 1♡, opener will be at least 5-4 in clubs-hearts *OR* 4-4-1-4 (singleton diamond). If it goes 1◇ : 1♡, 1♠, opener will be 4-1-4-4 (singleton heart) or have 4+ spades and 5+ diamonds. This should make your bidding more accurate since you do not have to factor in the chance of a 4-4-3-2 pattern.

2. Bidding after opener's 1NT rebid

Many play some version of 2♣ Checkback, but there is a better approach. It works particularly well when opener's 1NT rebid might have bypassed a major as in #1.

After the 1NT rebid, responder's 2♣ requires opener to bid 2◇. This is known as '2♣ puppet'. Responder might be intending to pass 2◇, but if responder takes another bid, that is natural and invites game. A 2◇ rebid after opener's 1NT rebid is artificial and forcing to game.

When using this together with opener's bypassing a major with the 1NT rebid, responder initially shows a 4-card major ahead of longer diamonds, unless strong enough to invite game.

```
        WEST              EAST
   ♠  J 7 6 2        ♠  8 5
   ♡  K 4            ♡  A Q 9 6
   ◇  Q 4 3          ◇  J 9 8 7 5 2
   ♣  A K Q 6        ♣  3

            West       East
            1♣         1♡
            1NT        2♣ (forces 2◇)
            2◇         No
```

East tries for a major suit contract with 1♡ and then signs off by using the 2♣ puppet. With enough to invite game responder can bid the diamonds first.

West	East
1♣	1♢
1NT	2♣ (forces 2♢)
2♢	2♡ ...

Any bid by responder, after the 2♣ puppet : 2♢, is natural and invites game. Here responder is showing diamonds and hearts and game-inviting values. Further bidding is natural.

West	East
1♣	1♢
1NT	2♢ ...

With enough for game, responder rebids 2♢. This is artificial and game-forcing. It is not a sign-off. To do that, responder would go through the 2♣ puppet. Bidding after the 2♢ game-force is natural.

There are many useful sequences using this approach:

West	East
1♣	1♠
1NT	2♡ ...

Responder has at least five spades – four hearts with no game-interest and wants to sign off in one of the majors.

West	East
1♣	1♠
1NT	2♣
2♢	2♡ ...

Responder has at least five spades – four hearts and is inviting game because the bidding went via the 2♣ puppet. With enough to insist on game, East would bid 2♢ over 1NT.

West	East
1♣	1♠
1NT	2♠ ...

Responder has at least five spades and no game interest.

West	East
1♣	1♠
1NT	2♣
2♢	2♠ ...

Responder has five spades and is inviting game.

West	East
1♣	1♠
1NT	2♣
2♢	3♠ ...

Responder has six spades and is inviting game.

West	East
1♣	1♡
1NT	2♣
2♢	2♠ ...

Responder is inviting game with four hearts and four spades.

West	East
1♣	1♡
1NT	2♣
2♢	2NT ...

Responder is inviting 3NT and has only four hearts.

West	East
1♣	1♡
1NT	2♣
2♢	3♣ ...

Responder is inviting game with four hearts and 4+ clubs.

The artificial game-forcing 2♢ rebid by responder is used for hands which are not especially shapely. With excellent shape, responder rebids with a jump to the three-level, which is also forcing to game. If bidding a new suit, the shape will be at least 5-5.

West	East
1♢	1♡
1NT	3♣ ...

Responder is forcing to game with 5+ hearts and 5+ clubs.

A jump to three of opener's suit also shows at least a 5-5:

West	East
1♣	1♠
1NT	3♣ ...

Responder is forcing to game with 5+ spades and 5+ clubs.

A jump to three of responder's suit shows a 7+ suit:

West	East
1♣	1♠
1NT	3♠ ...

Responder is forcing to game with 7+ spades. With only five or six spades, responder uses the artificial 2♢ rebid:

West	East
1♣	1♡
1NT	2♢
2♠	3♡ ...

Responder is forcing to game with six hearts. After the 2♢ rebid opener would show 3-card heart support with 2♡ ahead of showing the spade suit. As the 2♠ rebid by opener denied 3-card support East is now showing six hearts. Had East bid 3♠ over 2♠, that would show slam interest. Otherwise East would simply bid 4♠ over 2♠.

How can responder sign off in clubs? A 2♣ rebid after 1NT is a puppet to 2◊ and a continuation with 3♣ invites game. A jump to 3♣ after 1NT is game-forcing with a freakish hand. What about a very weak hand with long clubs or with club support for opener?

Just as one cannot stop in 2♣ after a 1NT opening if one is playing Stayman, so one cannot stop in 2♣ here. However, it is possible to stop in 3♣. Since we use a sequence like 1◊ : 1♡, 1NT : 2♣, 2◊ : 2NT to invite 3NT, the raise of 1NT to 2NT (say, 1◊ : 1♡, 1NT : 2NT) is not needed as an invitational raise. You can use the raise to 2NT as a puppet to 3♣. For example:

WEST	EAST	West	East
♠ A 2	♠ K 6 5 3	1◊	1♠
♡ Q J 6	♡ 4 3	1NT	2NT
◊ A K J 4 2	◊ 7	3♣	No
♣ 5 3 2	♣ Q J 8 7 6 4	Sign-off by East	

WEST	EAST	West	East
♠ A Q 2	♠ K 6 5 3	1♣	1♠
♡ Q 6 4	♡ 2	1NT	2NT
◊ A 9 2	◊ 7 6 5	3♣	No
♣ Q J 7 4	♣ K 10 5 3 2	Sign-off by East	

WEST	EAST	West	East
♠ A Q 2	♠ K J 5 3	1♣	1♠
♡ Q 6 4	♡ 9 2	1NT	2♣
◊ 9 8 5	◊ Q 6	2◊	3♣
♣ A Q J 4	♣ K 10 9 3 2	No	

Here East uses the 2♣ puppet to invite game, but West is minimum, with poor shape as well.

Showing three-suiters after a 1NT rebid

With no prospects for game, pass 1NT or bail out at the two-level if possible.

WEST	EAST	West	East
♠ 7 6	♠ Q J 8 5	1♣	1♡
♡ Q 6 4	♡ K 8 5 2	1NT	No
◇ A K 2	◇ 7 6 4 3		
♣ A Q J 4 2	♣ 3		

WEST	EAST	West	East
♠ 7 6	♠ Q J 8 5 3	1♣	1♠
♡ Q 6 4 3	♡ K 8 5 2	1NT	2♡
◇ A K 2	◇ 7 6 4 3	No	
♣ A Q J 4	♣ - - -		

As East did not use the 2♣ puppet to invite game or the 2◇ rebid to force to game, the 2♡ rebid shows a weak hand.

WEST	EAST	West	East
♠ A 6 2	♠ Q 7 5 3	1◇	1♡
♡ Q 6 4	♡ K 8 5 2	1NT	2♣
◇ A K 8 3	◇ J 6 4 2	2◇	No
♣ A 7 6	♣ 3		

West's 1NT shows 15-17 points. When playing a 12-14 or 11-14 1NT opening, the attractive rebid system is to use 1NT for 15-17 and a jump to 2NT with 18-19. This eliminates the ugly 3NT rebid on 19 points ('ugly' because it makes it very difficult to explore for the best game contract). Here East uses the 2♣ puppet to sign off in diamonds.

With enough to invite game, travel via the 2♣ puppet:

WEST	EAST	West	East
♠ 7 6 3	♠ Q J 8 5	1♣	1♡
♡ Q 6 4	♡ K 10 5 2	1NT	2♣
◇ A K 2	◇ Q J 6 5	2◇	2♠
♣ A K J 4	♣ 3	3NT	No

West's 1NT = 15-17. East's 2♠ rebid invites game, as East went via 2♣, and denies five hearts (failure to rebid 2♡).

With a three-suiter and enough for game responder can use the 2◇ game-force rebid, but if appropriate a natural reverse is usually more effective.

WEST	EAST	West	East
♠ A J 2	♠ K Q 5 3	1◇	1♡
♡ 8 6 4	♡ K Q 7 5	1NT	2♠
◇ A Q 8 3	◇ J 6 4 2	2NT	3◇
♣ A 7 6	♣ 3	3♡	5◇
		No	

East's 2♠ rebid is forcing to game and promises a three-suiter. West rebids 2NT to find the third suit. When East bids 3◇, thereby showing shortage in clubs, West's club holding makes 3NT unattractive (unless the partnership can run nine tricks). West's 3♡ shows 3-card heart support in case East is 4-5-4-0, but East is not eager to play the 4-3 fit.

WEST	EAST	West	East
♠ A J 2	♠ K Q 5 3	1◇	1♡
♡ 8 6 4	♡ K Q 7 5	1NT	2♠
◇ K Q 8 3	◇ J 6 4 2	2NT	3◇
♣ A Q 10	♣ 3	3NT	No

With powerful clubs, West is happy to play in 3NT.

WEST	EAST	West	East
♠ A 4 2	♠ K Q 5 3	1◇	1♡
♡ A J 4	♡ K Q 7 5	1NT	2♠
◇ 9 7 6 2	◇ 3	2NT	3♣
♣ A K 3	♣ J 7 4 2	3♡	4♡
		No	

When East bids 3♣, showing hearts, spades and clubs and therefore shortage in diamonds, West judges that 3NT could be risky (although it might succeed, of course). West shows 3-card heart support and with no trump fit elsewhere East settles for that game. If the opponents start by playing diamonds, East's best plan is a dummy reversal, aiming to ruff three diamonds in hand.

The multi-2◇ and rebids after the 2NT response

Among experts, the popularity of the multi-2◇ opening has grown, as that of Acol Twos and standard weak twos has waned. The multi-2◇ shows a weak two in hearts or a weak two in spades with (or sometimes without) some strong option.

The 2NT response is a strong inquiry with at least enough to invite game opposite a 6-10 point weak two. It used to be the fashion for opener then to show the suit and the strength, commonly using 3♣/3◇ to show hearts/spades and maximum values and 3♡/3♠ to show hearts/spades and a minimum, with 3NT showing A-K-Q-x-x-x in one of the majors.

One drawback to this approach is that the weak hand might become declarer when the reply to 2NT is 3♡ or 3♠. It is possible to eliminate this flaw without losing any benefits and at the same time improve your slam options. Perhaps you are already using this structure:

2◇ : 2NT, 3♣ = a weak two in hearts

2◇ : 2NT, 3◇ = a weak two in spades

The difference is that opener has not specified the range and has not bid the major suit held. With enough for game, but not slam, responder can bid game in opener's major. With a fit for opener's suit but only enough values to invite game, responder bids 3-of-opener's major (2◇ : 2NT, 3♣ : 3♡ or 2◇ : 2NT, 3◇ : 3♠). Opener passes if minimum or raises to game if maximum. Notice that in each case responder ends up as declarer.

With slam interest, responder makes the cheapest bid after opener has shown the major held (2◇ : 2NT, 3♣ : 3◇ or 2◇ : 2NT, 3◇ : 3♡). This sets opener's major as trumps and asks whether opener has a singleton. If so, opener bids the suit with the shortage. If not, opener bids 3NT. Again opener has not bid the major suit yet. Whether opener shows a shortage or rebids 3NT, any new suit now can be played as a cue-bid and 4NT as Roman Key Card Blackwood. Another option after a shortage has been shown is on page 38.

Using this approach, you can add a single-suited Acol Two in any suit and a powerful balanced hand as the strong options for the multi-2◇. The rebids after the 2NT inquiry then become:

2◇ : 2NT, 3♣ = a weak two in hearts
2◇ : 2NT, 3◇ = a weak two in spades
2◇ : 2NT, 3♡ = single-suiter, 9 playing tricks in hearts
2◇ : 2NT, 3♠ = single-suiter, 9 playing tricks in spades
2◇ : 2NT, 4♣ = Acol Two in clubs, single-suited
2◇ : 2NT, 4◇ = Acol Two in diamonds, single-suited
2◇ : 2NT, 3NT = 23-24 points, balanced

Balanced weak twos

Once you adopt the multi-2$\diamondsuit$, the question turns to how to use the 2$\heartsuit$ and 2$\spadesuit$ openings. One approach was to use them as Acol Twos, but you can see from the opposite page that this is not necessary for single-suited Acol Twos. You could use 2$\heartsuit$ or 2$\spadesuit$ for very strong two-suited hands, but these have very low frequency. Some use 2$\heartsuit$ / 2$\spadesuit$ to show five cards in the bid major and a 5-card undisclosed minor. Partner can ask for the minor with 2NT. The more daring open 2$\heartsuit$ / 2$\spadesuit$ with a 5-card major and a 4+ minor. There is obviously more risk attached to opening with a 5-4 pattern than with a 5-5, but to compensate for this the 5-4 holding has much greater frequency.

Two-suited 2$\heartsuit$ / 2$\spadesuit$ openings are in favour, but recently a new type of weak two has emerged: the balanced weak two.

2$\heartsuit$ = five hearts and a 5-3-3-2 or 5-4-2-2 pattern.

2$\spadesuit$ = five spades and a 5-3-3-2 or 5-4-2-2 pattern.

If opener is 5-4-2-2, the 4-carder will be a minor. The strength should be 9-11 HCP. These openings have two big pluses. Firstly, with a void or a singleton in opener's major, partner can run to a 5+ suit, knowing there will be at least doubleton support there and often 3-card support. Secondly, if the opponents intervene, it is much easier for partner to double for penalties since your hand is known to have reasonable strength and at least two cards in the suit overcalled.

With no game interest, responder passes with doubleton or better support. Raising the major to three is pre-emptive and a change of suit is an absolute sign-off.

With game interest, responder bids 2NT as a strong inquiry. Opener rebids 3♣ a strong suit in the major opened, one that can play opposite doubleton support. A 3♦ reply denies such a good quality suit, but promises three cards in the other major. Rebidding the major denies three cards in the other major and denies a very powerful major suit.

After the reply to 2NT any new suit by responder is natural and forcing. Opener can raise or support via a cue-bid.

If an opponent intervenes over the opening, a new suit by responder is forcing, double is penalties and a bid of opener's major at the three-level invites game.

Jump-raises of overcalls

The jump-raise of an overcall was once played as showing support and about the same strength as a minimum opening hand. This style has lost popularity among experts. This is a common, modern approach after they open, say, 1♦:

(1♦) : 1♠ : (No) : 2♠ = 6-9 points and 3-card spade support

(1♦) : 1♠ : (No) : 3♠ = 6-9 points and 4+ spade support

(1♦) : 1♠ : (No) : 2♦ = 10+ points and 3-card spade support

(1♦) : 1♠ : (No) : 3♦ = 10+ points and 4+ spade support

(1♦) : 1♠ : (No) : 2♦
(No) : 2♠ : (No) : ?

Partner's 2♠ shows a minimum overcall. You should pass this if also minimum, but raise to 3♠ with 13-14 points. Other bids are natural and game-tries with 13+ points. With a strong overcall, partner will make some bid other than 2♠.

The 3NT opening

If you are using the Gambling 3NT opening (long, solid minor with little else), you are welcome to it. If a prospective partner suggests we play the Gambling 3NT, I always say, 'Fine, but I will never open 3NT.'

The Gambling 3NT has too much downside. If 3NT is the right contract it is almost always played from the wrong side. Strong opponents know how to defend against it: lead an ace to take a look at dummy. Any weakness in dummy is then revealed and the defenders can easily exploit that weakness.

Prefer not have a 3NT opening at all than to play the Gambling 3NT. Once you reach that conclusion, you might be interested in using 3NT as a slam-going opening to ask for specific aces. Of course this makes it a rare opening, but it is extremely useful when it does arise.

3NT : 4♣ = no ace
3NT : 4♢, 4♡, 4♠, 5♣ = ace in the bid suit
3NT : 5♢, 5♡, 5♠, 6♣ = two aces, ace in the bid suit and ace in the next suit
3NT : 4NT = two non-touching aces
After the reply to 3NT, a suit bid is a sign-off and the cheapest no-trump bid asks for specific kings in like manner. For more details, see 'Kabel 3NT' in *Bridge Conventions, Defences and Countermeasures*, (Cassell/Peter Crawley). An example:

WEST	EAST	West	East
♠ A K Q J 6 3 2	♠ 4	3NT	5♣
♡ 4	♡ K Q 5 3 2	6♠	No
♢ - - -	♢ J 6 5 4 2	(5♣ = the ♣A
♣ K Q J 8 3	♣ A 5	and no other ace.)

Slam exploration after partner has shown a shortage

In many modern methods one partner or the other can show a singleton or a void in a specific suit. It might be combined with showing good trump support as with a splinter bid. A splinter bid is an unnecessary jump, such as 1♠ : 4◇, and shows 4+ trump support and shortage in the suit bid. Opener can also make a splinter bid, such as 1♠ : 2♡, 4♣, which shows 4+ heart support and a singleton or void in clubs. These splinter bids are game-forcing and slam invitations.

Another possibility is that the shortage is shown in reply to a specific inquiry or game-forcing bid. A popular treatment these days is to use the 2NT response not in a natural sense of a balanced 11-12 points, but as a game-forcing raise of opener's major (Jacoby 2NT). It promises 4+ support and normally 13+ points. In reply, a new suit by opener shows shortage in that suit. Without any shortage, opener repeats the major or bids 3NT, depending on the values and trump length held. For example:

Opener	Responder		
1♡	2NT	2NT	= game-force raise in hearts
3♠ ...		3♠	= singleton or void in spades

After the multi-2◇, responder with a fit for opener's suit and slam interest can ask if opener has a shortage (page 34).

Opener	Responder		
2◇	2NT	2NT	= strong inquiry
3♣	3◇	3♣	= weak two in hearts
4♣ ...		3◇	= 'Do you have a short suit?'
		4♣	= 'Yes, in clubs.'

The question is, what happens next after the shortage has been shown? One approach is to use cue-bids and 4NT as Roman Key Card Blackwood. That is fine, but this approach has much to recommend it:

Immediately after the shortage has been shown, the cheapest bid is an inquiry as to strength and whether a singleton or a void is held. In reply to the ask, the cheapest bid says, 'I am minimum', the next step = 'I have extras and a singleton' and the third step = 'I have extras and a void.'

If partner bids step 1 to show a minimum, the cheapest step inquires further and in reply, first step = singleton, second step = void. After the singleton or void has been clarified, the cheapest bid is Roman Key Card Blackwood. Here are some examples:

Opener	Responder	
1♠	2NT	2NT = game-force raise in spades
3♢	3♡	3♢ = short in diamonds, 3♡ asks
3♠	3NT	3♠ = minimum, 3NT asks
4♣	4♢ ...	4♣ = singleton diamond
		4♢ = RKCB
1♡	2NT	2NT = game-force raise in hearts
3♢	3♡	3♢ = short in diamonds, 3♡ asks
3NT	4♣ ...	3NT = non-minimum, singleton in diamonds, 4♣ = RKCB
1♡	2NT	2NT = game-force raise in hearts
3♢	3♡	3♢ = short in diamonds, 3♡ asks
4♣	4♢ ...	4♣ = non-minimum and void in diamonds, 4♢ = RKCB

When using this approach, 3NT can be used as an asking bid if a major suit has been agreed. If a minor suit is trumps, 3NT is to play. In that case, if the cheapest ask would be 3NT, use 4♣ as the next asking bid.

Game in the agreed suit by the asker is a sign-off, never an ask. If the cheapest ask would be game in the trump suit, use the first bid beyond trumps as the next ask. For example:

Opener	Responder	
1♥	3♠	3♠ = heart raise, short in spades
3NT	4◇	3NT asks, 4◇ = non-minimum and
?		a singleton in spades, not a void

As 4♥ would be a sign-off, use 4♠ here as RKCB.

Some pairs show key cards immediately when a void is held. This is sensible and just requires a little more memory work. For example:

Opener	Responder	
1♥	2NT	2NT = game-force raise in hearts
3◇	3♥	3◇ = short in diamonds, 3♥ asks
?		

Opener's reply to the 3♥ ask:
3♠ = minimum opening
3NT = non-minimum, singleton in diamonds
4♣ = non minimum, diamond void, 0 or 3 key cards
4◇ = non-minimum, diamond void, 1 or 4 key cards
4♥ = non-minimum, diamond void, 2 key cards, no ♥Q
4♠ = non-minimum, diamond void, 2 key cards + the ♥Q

The extra bids here save a step, but you can play the shortage inquiry perfectly well without using the void run-on steps.

After partner has shown a shortage, bidding game in the trump suit is intended as a sign-off and the cheapest other bid is the asking bid. What about a new suit bid other than either of these? The need for such a bid would arise rarely, but if it occurs it is used as a cue-bid and is often a void. Take a look at this deal:

Dealer North : Game all

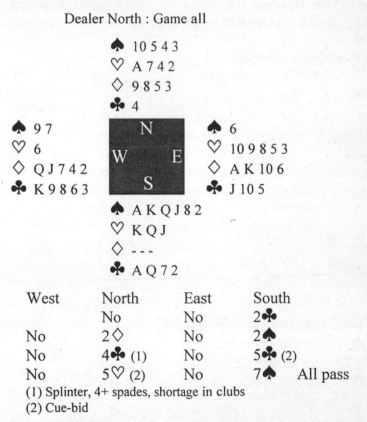

| ♠ 10 5 4 3 |
| ♡ A 7 4 2 |
| ◇ 9 8 5 3 |
| ♣ 4 |

♠ 9 7		♠ 6
♡ 6		♡ 10 9 8 5 3
◇ Q J 7 4 2		◇ A K 10 6
♣ K 9 8 6 3		♣ J 10 5

| ♠ A K Q J 8 2 |
| ♡ K Q J |
| ◇ - - - |
| ♣ A Q 7 2 |

West	North	East	South
	No	No	2♣
No	2◇	No	2♠
No	4♣ (1)	No	5♣ (2)
No	5♡ (2)	No	7♠ All pass

(1) Splinter, 4+ spades, shortage in clubs
(2) Cue-bid

After the 4♣ splinter, South can see a small slam and a grand slam is possible if North has the ♡A. Using the 4◇ ask after 4♣ will not solve the problem and so South starts a cue-bidding auction. North's 5♡ solves South's problem.

What happens after the reply to RKCB?

Roman Key Card Blackwood is the slam bidding inquiry of
choice for almost all experts. The major benefit is that it
allows the partnership to locate not just the aces, but also the
king and queen of trumps. The trump king is treated as equal
to an ace. The four aces and the trump king are known as the
'key cards'. The replies to 4NT are:

5♣ = 0 or 3 key cards
5♦ = 1 or 4 key cards
5♥ = two key cards but not the trump queen
5♠ = two key cards and the trump queen

After the 5♣ or 5♦ reply, the cheapest bid excluding the
trump suit (which is a sign-off) asks, 'Do you have the trump
queen?' Partner replies with the cheapest bid, 'No' and the
next bid for 'Yes'. For more information about RKCB, see
Bridge Conventions, Defences and Countermeasures.

What happens after the key cards and the trump queen have
been located? If you know the right spot, simply bid it, but if
a grand slam is feasible you will often need more information.
Some use the 5NT rebid to ask for kings, but a more popular
use is to ask partner to bid the cheapest king outside trumps.
Which king is held is often more important than how many.

What about a new suit bid beyond five of the agreed trump
suit? This can be used as an asking bid for the king and queen
in that suit (not the ace as that was included in the reply to
RKCB). The answers are straightforward:

Cheapest bid = no queen, no king
Next step = queen, but not the king
Step 3 = king, but not the queen
Step 4 = king and queen

Consider this deal:

Dealer North : Love all

```
              ♠ A 10 7
              ♡ 3
              ◇ K Q 9 5 2
              ♣ A 8 5 3
♠ 8 2                              ♠ J 6 3
♡ J 10 8 7 4      N               ♡ Q 9 6 2
◇ 6 3        W         E          ◇ J 8 7 4
♣ Q 9 4 2         S               ♣ J 10
              ♠ K Q 9 5 4
              ♡ A K 5
              ◇ A 10
              ♣ K 7 6
```

West	North	East	South
	1◇	No	1♠
No	2♠	No	4NT
No	5♡ (1)	No	6◇ (2)
No	7♣ (3)	No	7♠ All pass

(1) Two key cards, no ♠Q
(2) Asking bid in diamonds
(3) 'I have the ◇K and ◇Q.'

After the 5♡ reply, South asks in diamonds as the ◇K is needed for any decent chance for a grand slam. The deal arose in the 2005 World Championships (Round 18, Board 1). There were 22 teams in each of the Bermuda Bowl (Open Teams), Venice Cup (Women's Teams) and the Seniors Bowl. Of the 66 pairs holding these cards, 39 bid and made 7♠. One failed in 7♣, three failed in 7NT, one stopped in 4♠ and all the others were in 6♠.

The previous deal was slightly flawed, since a bad spade break might defeat it, but this one is outstanding:

Dealer South : Love all

```
                    ♠ Q J 8 4 3
                    ♡ A
                    ◇ A
                    ♣ A Q J 10 7 6
    ♠ 7                   N              ♠ 6 5
    ♡ 5 3                                ♡ K J 8 2
    ◇ K Q 10 8 7 6 3 2   W     E         ◇ J 9 4
    ♣ 3 2                 S              ♣ 9 8 5 4
                    ♠ A K 10 9 2
                    ♡ Q 10 9 7 6 4
                    ◇ 5
                    ♣ K
```

West	North	East	South
			1♡
4◇	Dble (1)	No	4♠
No	4NT	No	5♡ (2)
No	6♣ (3)	No	6♠ (4)
No	7♠	All pass	

(1) For takeout
(2) Two key cards, no ♠Q
(3) Asking bid in clubs
(4) 'I have the ♣K, but not the ♣Q.'

This also arose in the 2005 World Championships and 7♠ or 7NT should be reached. Of the 66 pairs, nine played in 7NT and 31 were in 7♠. There were 17 in 6♠, five in 6♣, one each in 4♣, 4♠ and 5♠ and one failed in 7♡. This was another sensible auction after South chose a 1♠ opening:

West	North	East	South
			1♠
4◇	4NT	No	5♡
No	5NT (1)	No	6♣ (2)
No	7♠	All pass	

(1) Asking for specific kings
(2) 'I have the ♣K.'

Note how essential it is to locate a specific king. If North's 5NT simply asked for kings and South showed one, North would not know whether it was the vital ♣K or the useless ♡K.

5NT as 'pick a slam'

After the reply to 4NT, a 5NT bid usually asks for kings, either the number of kings or specific kings. What about a 5NT bid not preceded by 4NT? In some cases this is a grand slam inquiry, asking about the number of top trumps held out of the ace, king and queen. What if there has been no agreement as to a trump suit? Many pairs then use 5NT to ask partner to pick a small slam. For example:

WEST	EAST	West	East
♠ A K 3	♠ Q J 6	2NT	3♣
♡ K 8 2	♡ Q 4	3◇	5NT
◇ K Q 6	◇ A 7 4 3	6♣	No
♣ A Q 9 8	♣ K J 5 2		

3◇ = no 5-card major; 5NT = pick a slam. You would be lucky to make 6NT, but 6♣ is excellent.

Chapter 4

Strategy

One of the vital items on your agenda for discussion with partner is your general strategy in a number of situations. This is often expressed in terms of 'expectation'. When partner makes an overcall, what is expected? Must it be a good suit or is a poor suit acceptable if the hand is strong?

Make sure to discuss your style with takeout doubles. Should a minimum takeout double of one major promise four cards in the other major? At what strength is it reasonable to hold only three cards in the other major?

Suppose you make a takeout double and partner bids one in a major. What strength is expected from you if you raise to two of the major? Some players raise with a minimum double simply to confirm 4-card support and to make it a little tougher for the opponents to compete. Others expect a strong hand if the doubler bids again.

You must sort out which sequences are constructive, perhaps invitational, and which ones are simply competitive or just pre-emptive. If the bidding starts 1♠ : 2♠, is opener's bid of 3♠ an invitation to game or is it pre-emptive and aimed at keeping the opponents out of the auction? You can play it either way, but make sure you know which way it is.

Another important area is the partnership style for pre-empts. How good a suit should one have for a three-opening? Is a pathetic suit acceptable at favourable vulnerability or should the suit itself always be respectable?

As long as partner knows that your three-openings can be total rubbish at favourable vulnerability, you can occasionally pull off a triumph such as this:

Dealer East : North-South vulnerable

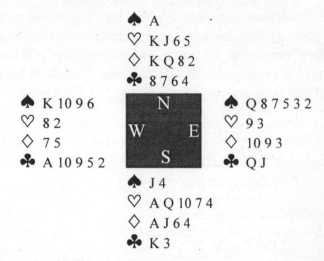

```
                    ♠ A
                    ♡ K J 6 5
                    ◇ K Q 8 2
                    ♣ 8 7 6 4
♠ K 10 9 6                          ♠ Q 8 7 5 3 2
♡ 8 2          N                    ♡ 9 3
◇ 7 5       W     E                 ◇ 10 9 3
♣ A 10 9 5 2      S                 ♣ Q J
                    ♠ J 4
                    ♡ A Q 10 7 4
                    ◇ A J 6 4
                    ♣ K 3
```

At one table in an international match on Bridge Base Online in 2007 the bidding went:

West	North	East	South
		3♠	No
4♠	No	No	No

Declarer was two down for –100. Perhaps North or South might have taken action, but it was difficult. At the other table:

West	North	East	South
		2◇ (1)	2♡
No	4♡	No	No
4♠	5♡	All pass	

(1) Multi

Declarer made eleven tricks for +650 and +11 Imps.

You court trouble when your action is outside the range of partner's expectation. This deal arose in a national teams event in 2007:

Dealer West : East-West vulnerable

```
                    ♠ J 8 4 3
                    ♡ A Q 10 5 4 2
                    ◇ 8 4
                    ♣ J
♠ K                                      ♠ A 9 7 5
♡ J 8 6            N                      ♡ 7 3
◇ 9 7 3         W     E                   ◇ A J 10 6 5
♣ A 10 8 6 4 2     S                      ♣ 7 5
                    ♠ Q 10 6 2
                    ♡ K 9
                    ◇ K Q 2
                    ♣ K Q 9 3
```

West	North	East	South
3♣	3♡	No	3NT
No	No	Dble	All pass

No doubt East was expecting a much better suit for a 3♣ opening at unfavourable vulnerability. East could see South would be in trouble if West had, say, ♣A-Q-J-x-x-x-x.

West led the ♣6, won in dummy. Declarer played a low spade from dummy and East rose with the ♠A to play a club through South. The defence made just three aces and South had +650. If East had suspected West could open 3♣ with this motley lot, East would pass. Moral: Make sure you and partner agree on the appropriate values for the various actions you might be taking.

Chapter 5

At a tournament

How can you improve your performance once you are at the tournament itself? First and foremost, arrive early, at least ten minutes before the session is due to start. You will be experiencing anxiety if you are running late. You do not need that. If you are not there five minutes before session time, partner starts having a panic attack. Partner will be wondering whether something has happened to you, are you in an accident, and so on. If not concerned about your welfare, partner will at least be angry that you are so inconsiderate to be late. Neither anxiety nor anger will improve partner's game.

Here is an even better idea. Athletes always warm up before they are about to race. So do footballers, so do others involved in sport. If its good for sports people, why not for bridge players? Turn up half an hour before play and bring a couple of packs of cards. Sit down in a quiet spot with your partner and do some bidding practice on half a dozen hands. Then your little grey cells will already be firing at session start.

Also make sure you have brought your system cards with you. It is irritating if you have to sit down and complete a new system card just before play begins. Both partners should carry a set of system cards. That way if one happens to forget, the other should have a set.

Another sensible move is to drink a glass of water just before the start of the session. Even though you are playing bridge, dehydration is a factor. Dehydrated players tire more easily and tiredness brings on a loss of concentration.

Drinking water during the session is also important. Have a glass of water every 40-60 minutes. It will refresh you. Make sure that the water is room temperature or close to it. Avoid ice cold water. Why is that? Because the stomach will need energy to warm the water and will take blood from your brain cells to do it. For a few minutes after drinking ice water you are not as alert as you could be. If the venue has only ice water, mix the ice water with hot water (usually available for coffees or teas). About 80% ice water and 20% boiling water brings the mixture to the right temperature.

During each session there are a few things you can do to help partner. If you are dummy, always put down the good news first. Partner will have some anxiety as to what will appear and seeing the good part will reduce that anxiety more quickly. It might be only by a few seconds, but long term you might be adding a few weeks to your partner's life.

Another good habit: Put down last the suit of the opening lead. That will force partner to look at the other suits first and might prevent partner playing too quickly from dummy.

Do you say, 'Thank you' when dummy appears? If you do, then you must say it every time. Otherwise when you do not, partner might imagine that you are not satisfied with the contents of dummy. It is tempting to make clever comments ('Whatever happened to the hand you held during the bidding, partner?'), but anything that could belittle partner must be avoided.

Above all, refrain from any possible criticism during the session. It is better not to have any discussion at all during session time. Save it for after the session has ended.

The only time some conversation is needed is if you have had a horrible misunderstanding. Perhaps you took partner's bid as weak and partner meant it as strong. All you need say is something like, "Let's discuss it later. For the rest of this session, why don't we play it your way?"

Partners do not suddenly play better if you rebuke them. If they have done something silly, they almost certainly know that already. They will not feel better if you point it out to them. Try to say something sympathetic and if that is not possible, keep quiet. As in other areas of your life, if you cannot say something nice, say nothing.

If you feel an irresistible urge to scream after some huge blunder, excuse yourself from the table, go to the bathroom and splash cold water over your face. That will give you time to cool down and regain your composure. The same solution is helpful if you are the one who has blundered.

Despite all the evidence that might possibly be to the contrary, partner is on your side and is doing his best. None of us is free of error. Mistakes are like car headlights: the other guy's only seem more glaring than our own. You will not win any friends if you resort to sarcastic comments: "Partner, every day you are playing worse and worse, but today you are playing like next Friday."

Partners who feel that you have confidence in them will play as well as they are able. It is bad enough that partner has made one mistake and produced a bad board. If they are stung by your remarks, they will almost certainly play worse, in the short term anyway, and instead of one bad board you will have two or three bad results.

Suppose your trump suit is:

♠ J 9 8 4

♠ A K Q 10 7

You are about to ruff in hand. Which card do you choose?

Of course, it makes no difference to you. All your trumps are high, but you should ruff with the ace. This will reduce any anxiety partner might have. If you can afford to ruff with the ace, obviously all is well. Ruffing so high can also have an intimidating affect on the opponents. They might think, 'If declarer can afford to ruff with the ace, what chance do we have?' If you regularly ruff with the ace in such situations rather than with an equal lower trump, you will gradually acquire a reputation as a flamboyant player and there is nothing wrong with that.

A bridge session demands a high level of concentration for a number of hours. Here is one of the best tips of all: when you are dummy, tune out. Relax. Do not follow the play except insofar as is necessary to stop partner from revoking or playing from the wrong hand. Reduce your focus from fierce concentration to just above snoozing.

By doing this you will conserve your energy and be a little more refreshed for the next deal. Why waste energy where it cannot gain you instead of saving it for a future deal when you might have a tough play or defensive problem?

Reality is often quite the opposite. Players concentrate twice as hard when dummy so that when the deal is over they can point out where partner went wrong. This is dumb on so many counts.

What if partner makes a disparaging comment to you? It is not in your best interests to enter into an argument there and then as to who was right or wrong. A good strategy is to get up and leave the table, go to the bathroom and again splash water over your face. If you do this repeatedly when partner is critical, partner will soon learn that to do so is a waste of time and eventually will not bother.

Even if you feel in your heart and soul that you are absolutely right in your decision, do not become involved in an argument or even a discussion at the table. Nothing good ever comes of it. In addition it might turn out later that your absolute belief was in fact not correct. Partner might have had perfectly valid reasons for the action taken, even though it seemed to you to be a blunder at the time.

There are some partners who cannot help being critical. Some very strong players choose to attack partner as soon as play ends before it becomes obvious that they themselves have made the mistake. It is best to find another partner.

Some partners can do no wrong, in their own mind, that is. Whenever you have a bad result, you will always be told it is your fault. You do not need that kind of partner either.

In addition to relaxing as dummy and regular glasses of water, there are other ways to ensure a high level of concentration. If you are having a meal before a session or between sessions, try to finish eating at least one hour before the start of the next session. A full belly makes for a full brain. While food is being digested, the stomach needs more blood and so the brain has less. Also watch what you eat before a session. Foods high in starch have a tendency to make you sleepy. Prefer a meal with more protein than starch and avoid fatty meals.

As for alcohol before or during a session, that is a no-no. Some players need alcohol so that they can have an excuse for playing below par. Others feel it does no harm. Alcohol will not make you play better. It might help you not feel too bad about playing poorly. Alcohol in your bloodstream will impair your judgment. Why do you think drink-driving is a crime? Under the influence of alcohol you will find that you make mistakes which are totally out of character, blunders you would never make if you were fully alert. You do not need this.

Traces of alcohol can stay in the bloodstream for 24 hours (or longer, depending on how much you have had). It follows that the best strategy of all is to stay alcohol-free during the tournament if you can. Let the others enjoy their drinks with their meal and after the session is over. You can have yours at your victory celebration.

After a meal or between sessions, take a walk in the fresh air. That will make you brighter for the start of the next session. Another option is a brief nap if that is possible. Make sure you have an alarm or a partner to wake you in good time .

Suppose you are playing in a teams tournament and you and partner have the session off. What should you do? Unless there is no further play that day, try to find some way to relax. As above, a good walk or some sleep is useful. At major events there will be a Viewgraph theatre available. To watch a Viewgraph session can be very draining. Attend them only if you are off for the last session of a day. Avoid them if you might be playing in the next session that day. Discuss deals with partner if you are off for the day's last session. Do not do so if you have another session coming up that day. Relax.

The most important factor during a long tournament is sleep. You must get your full quota of sleep each night. There is hardly anything more refreshing than a good night's sleep.

This might not be so easy when you have so much adrenalin pumping through your body because of the excitement of the event. Try not to use sleeping pills, but it is better to take a pill to sleep than to lie awake for long periods rehashing the day's deals. As far as you can, use sleeping pills that do not have drowsy effects next day. If you have had a bad night's sleep, try to nap between sessions next day.

What about sex during a long tournament? There is nothing wrong with having sex as long as it does not interfere with your sleep requirements. If you want to play bridge at your best, it is silly to party all night during a tournament. It might bring pleasure, but your bridge will also suffer if most of the night is spent in sexual activities. As bridge is a partnership game, you owe it to your partner, and your team-mates, to be in good shape for each session. Consider your priorities.

It is not easy to concentrate fully all the time. It is a strain on your mental capacity. You need to remember the bidding and each card that is played for a period of about six minutes and when the deal is over, you have to wipe your mental slate clean and do it all again on the next deal.

Do you ever find that you missed a vital card that partner or declarer has played? Almost all of us do that sometime or other. What has happened is a loss of concentration. Perhaps you can reduce the frequency of missed cards by adopting a mantra. When the opening lead is made, repeat to yourself, 'Watch the cards, watch the cards, watch the cards'.

You can also reduce the workload by studying the system played by the opponents. If each round is short, two or three boards, you will do this only at the start of the round. When you are playing a long match, you should study their system in advance, especially their card play agreements. Their leads and signalling will tend to be true more often than if they see you studying their system card as play is under way.

If partners want discussion after the session is over, focus only on matters of bidding and the defensive problems. Do not discuss any of partner's declarer play hands. Bidding is partnership business, defence is partnership business, but declarer play is personal. If partner wants your opinion about a hand they played, they will ask you. If you are not asked, do not offer advice. If they do ask you, it is a good idea to start by saying, 'Sorry, I was not watching the play. What happened?' Remember the earlier advice that when partner is declarer you should relax and not follow the play at all.

When it is time to score up in a teams event, you should be present even if you were not playing that session. That builds team bonding. Never ask team-mates what happened on a deal where they obtained a terrible result. The best approach is to do the scoring in full, with nothing being said other than calling out the scores. When that is finished, each pair should leave and discuss their own problems in private. If you wish to boost your team-mates morale, ask them how they achieved their very good results. They will be chuffed.

Finally, never humiliate your partner in public or in private. It is extremely poor form to regale your friends with stories how partner butchered any number of deals. Such behaviour will eventually find its way back to partner.

Chapter 6

Bidding Quiz

The problems in all the quizzes come mainly from recent international events or from national championships. Assume the setting is teams bridge unless stated otherwise.

When there is no opposition bidding, the main issue in bidding is hand valuation and judgment. When a good trump fit exists, the Losing Trick Count is a more accurate method for valuing your hand than any point count method. Always trust your partner in the bidding and co-operate if partner is trying for a game or a slam.

When the auction becomes competitive, there are many more problems to solve. Should you be aiming for penalties? Should you bid one more? A lot of competitive decisions are about whether you have the courage to take a certain action.

There are lots of options for doubles, including not just the simple takeout double or the negative double, but also the responsive double, the lead-directing double, the convertible values double, the support double and more.

New ideas are constantly evolving and prominent are methods for showing two-suiters. The Unusual 2NT and Michaels Cue-Bid are well known, but now we also have Leaping Michaels (jumps to the four-level after a weak two opening or after a multi-2♦ opening). A modern strain of the weak two is used to show a two-suited hand and even more recent is a weak 2♡ or 2♠ guaranteeing a 5332 or a 5422 pattern.

1. Dealer East : N-S vulnerable

West	North	East	South
		1♠	2NT (1)
No	3◇	No	?

(1) At least 5-5 minors, any strength

What would you do next as South with:

♠ ---
♡ A 6 5
◇ A K Q 9 2
♣ Q 8 7 6 2

(Solution on page 59)

2. Dealer South : Game all

West	North	East	South
			2♡ (1)
2♠	?		

(1) Weak, 6-10, 5 hearts and a 4+ minor

What would you do as North with:

♠ 8 6 2
♡ J 8 7 4 2
◇ A 4 2
♣ J 7

(Solution on page 60)

3. Dealer East : N-S vulnerable

West	North	East	South
		2♠ (1)	No
3♠	4NT (2)	No	5◇
5♡	?		

(1) 5-card weak two   (2) Shows both minors

What would you do now as North with:

♠ 5
♡ 10 2
◇ A Q J 6 2
♣ A K 9 8 4

(Solution on page 61)

4. Dealer East : Game all

West	North	East	South
		No	1◇
No	?		

What should North do with:

♠ K Q J
♡ J 5 2
◇ Q J 8 6
♣ 6 3 2

(Solution on page 62)

Solutions:

1.   Dealer East : North-South vulnerable

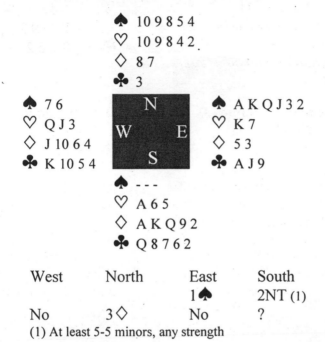

	♠ 109854		
	♡ 109842		
	◇ 87		
	♣ 3		

♠ 76   ♠ AKQJ32
♡ QJ3   ♡ K7
◇ J1064   ◇ 53
♣ K1054   ♣ AJ9

♠ ---
♡ A65
◇ AKQ92
♣ Q8762

West	North	East	South
		1♠	2NT (1)
No	3◇	No	?

(1) At least 5-5 minors, any strength

Source: 2005 World Championships, Round 1. The Unusual 2NT overcall is normally a weak bid, but some play it as a wide-ranging action. With 15 HCP and only 4½ losers South is worth another move. A raise to 4◇ seems attractive, but if you feel like doing that, you might as well bid 3♡ to show your complete pattern. Partner will be happy to pass and 3♡ is not nearly as expensive as any excursion in diamonds.

Scores included 5◇, 4◇, 3◇ doubled, 3NT E-W making and 4♠ failing. Each division had 22 teams. Datums (average): Open E-W 340, Women's E-W 260, Seniors E-W 290.

2.   Dealer South : Game all

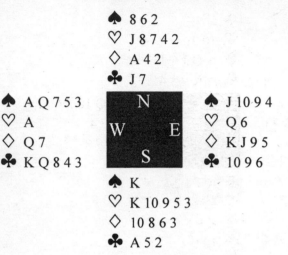

♠ 8 6 2
♡ J 8 7 4 2
◇ A 4 2
♣ J 7

♠ A Q 7 5 3
♡ A
◇ Q 7
♣ K Q 8 4 3

♠ J 10 9 4
♡ Q 6
◇ K J 9 5
♣ 10 9 6

♠ K
♡ K 10 9 5 3
◇ 10 8 6 3
♣ A 5 2

Source: 2005 World Championships, Round 1. At virtually every table East-West played in 4♠. Datums in all three divisions was E-W 640. At one table it went:

West	North	East	South
			2♡ (1)
2♠	No!	No	No

(1) Weak, 6-10, five hearts and a 4+ minor

North can tell that East-West are very likely to have game somewhere and the natural inclination is a pre-emptive jump in hearts. Rather than silence the opponents, this can help them judge their assets and their heart shortage. With almost no chance of winning the auction, silence can be best in the hope that partner's weak opening has already done its work.

East-West could have done better, of course. East might have raised to 3♠ and with only four losers, West is definitely worth a Leaping Michaels 4♣ (5 clubs and 5 spades).

3.   Dealer East : North-South vulnerable

```
                        ♠ 5
                        ♡ 10 2
                        ◇ A Q J 6 2
                        ♣ A K 9 8 4

    ♠ J 8 3              N              ♠ K Q 10 7 6
    ♡ A Q 9 8 7 6     W     E           ♡ K J 4
    ◇ 4                                 ◇ 10 7 3
    ♣ Q 7 3              S              ♣ J 6

                        ♠ A 9 4 2
                        ♡ 5 3
                        ◇ K 9 8 5
                        ♣ 10 5 2
```

West	North	East	South
		2♠	No
3♠	4NT	No	5◇
5♡	No??	No	6◇
No	No	Dble	All pass

Source: Teams match on Bridge Base Online, 2007. South lost two hearts and a club for –500. With North bidding 4NT at unfavourable vulnerability, it was clear that the hand belonged to North-South. South took North's pass of 5♡ as forcing and hence a slam invitation. With significantly more than he might have had, South went on 6◇ for a disastrous outcome. With 3½ quick tricks North should double 5♡. Although North has no trump tricks, the double warns partner not to bid further. Against 5♡ doubled the defence can collect 500 easily and 800 double dummy. As the cards lie, East-West do better to play in 5♠ doubled.

4.   Dealer East : Game all

♠ K Q J
♡ J 5 2
◇ Q J 8 6
♣ 6 3 2

♠ 10 8 6 5 4 2
♡ 8 4
◇ K
♣ K 10 9 5

♠ 9 7 3
♡ K Q 9 6 3
◇ 10 4 2
♣ J 8

♠ A
♡ A 10 7
◇ A 9 7 5 3
♣ A Q 7 4

Source: 2005 World Championships, Round 2. The North hand has 10 HCP, no major and support for diamonds. That might suggest a jump to 3◇ as a 10-12 point limit raise, but 3◇ is too much for the North cards. You should downgrade a hand for a 4-3-3-3 pattern and unsupported jacks are not worth the full one point value we give them. Just as it is recommended to add one point for holding all four aces, it is sensible to deduct one point for holding four jacks.

Not only should a limit raise be 10-12 points, but it should also be an 8-loser hand. The North hand has 9 losers, which is typical for a single raise. Likewise if North-South play inverted minors, the North hand is worth 3◇, showing about 6-9 points, rather than the forcing 2◇ raise of 10+ points.

After a 3◇ limit raise South might look for slam. Nine of the 66 pairs perished in 6◇, thirteen played in 5◇ and 41, almost two-thirds, were in the best spot of 3NT.

5. Dealer West : Game all

West	North	East	South
1♠	Dble	2♠	Dble
No	?		

(Solution on page 64)

What would you do next as North with:

♠ 3
♡ K Q 9 2
◇ A J 10 3
♣ Q 10 9 3

6. Dealer East : N-S vulnerable

West	North	East	South
		No	1♣ (1)
1♠ (2)	No	3♠ (3)	4♡
4♠	?		

(1) 15+ HCP, any shape
(2) Spades and clubs
(3) Pre-emptive

(Solution on page 65)

What would you do as North with:

♠ Q 4 2
♡ 8 7 6 4
◇ K 10 6 5
♣ J 10

7. Dealer South : E-W vulnerable

West	North	East	South
			No
1♠	Dble	No	1NT
No	?		

(Solution on page 66)

What would you do now as North with:

♠ 6
♡ A J 9
◇ A 10 9 8 2
♣ A Q 7 3

8. Dealer South : Game all

West	North	East	South
			1♡
No	1♠	No	2♡
No	3♣	No	?

(Solution on page 67)

What should South do with:

♠ A 2
♡ K Q J 10 3 2
◇ Q 4
♣ 8 7 2

5.   Dealer West : Game all

```
                    ♠ 3
                    ♡ K Q 9 2
                    ◇ A J 10 3
                    ♣ Q 10 9 3
```

```
♠ K Q J 10 7 5        N          ♠ A 6 4
♡ 4                              ♡ 8 7 6 5 3
◇ 7 4           W         E      ◇ K 9 5
♣ K J 5 2             S          ♣ 7 4
```

```
                    ♠ 9 8 2
                    ♡ A J 10
                    ◇ Q 8 6 2
                    ♣ A 8 6
```

West	North	East	South
1♠	Dble	2♠	Dble
No	2NT (1)	No	3◇
No	No	No	

(1) 'Scramble': Pick a minor, please.

Source: 2005 World Championships, Round 2. South's double here says, 'I have the values to bid at the next level, but it is not clear which suit I should bid.' The 'responsive' double, after third player raises opener's suit after a takeout double, often shows two suits of the same rank, both majors after a minor suit opening, both minors after a major suit opening.

If North has to guess which minor to bid, North might choose 3♣, which fails. North's 2NT asks South to pick the minor. That way North-South end in 3◇, which can succeed. If East-West bid on to 3♠, so be it.

If West opens 3♠, East should pass and not raise to 4♠.

6.   Dealer East : North-South vulnerable

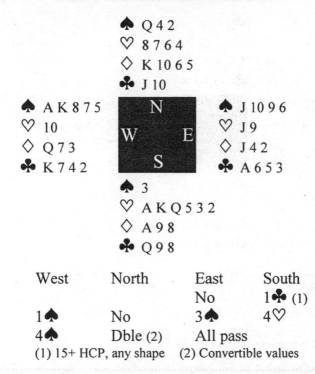

```
              ♠ Q 4 2
              ♡ 8 7 6 4
              ◇ K 10 6 5
              ♣ J 10
♠ A K 8 7 5      N         ♠ J 10 9 6
♡ 10          W     E      ♡ J 9
◇ Q 7 3          S         ◇ J 4 2
♣ K 7 4 2                  ♣ A 6 5 3
              ♠ 3
              ♡ A K Q 5 3 2
              ◇ A 9 8
              ♣ Q 9 8
```

West	North	East	South
		No	1♣ (1)
1♠	No	3♠	4♡
4♠	Dble (2)	All pass	

(1) 15+ HCP, any shape   (2) Convertible values

Source: 2005 World Championships, Round 6. There is a natural temptation for North to bid 5♡ over 4♠, but that is not sound. There is no assurance that the five-level is safe (even 4♡ was already too high). North's double says, 'Do what's right. Bid on with significant extra strength or shape, else let's play 4♠ doubled.' South has no reason to bid on.

In the world championships nine N-S pairs made 4♡ (a shift to diamonds by either defender is fatal for the defence), 18 collected 300 from 4♠ doubled, 13 collected less from 4♠ undoubled, eight failed in 4♡, nine were –200 in 5♡ and two were in 5♡ doubled.

7.   Dealer South : East-West vulnerable

```
              ♠ 6
              ♡ A J 9
              ◇ A 10 9 8 2
              ♣ A Q 7 3
♠ Q J 10 5 3        N        ♠ 9 8 7
♡ K Q 10 7 3    W       E    ♡ 6 5 4
◇ K 7                        ◇ Q 6 4
♣ K                 S        ♣ 10 9 4 2
              ♠ A K 4 2
              ♡ 8 2
              ◇ J 5 3
              ♣ J 8 6 5
```

West	North	East	South
			No
1♠	Dble	No	1NT
No	2NT	No	3NT
No	No	No	

Source: 2005 World Championships, Round 6. Should North pass 1NT or raise to 2NT? The 1NT response to a takeout double is generally played as 6-10 HCP and no unbid 4-card major. With 15 points, the doubler might pass 1NT, but the North hand is closer to 17 points than 15 and so a raise to 2NT is justified, even though North-South are not vulnerable. If four aces are worth one extra point, three aces are almost as good and you should allow an extra point for the decent 5-card diamond suit. 3NT is an easy make.

Of the 66 tables, 27 North-South pairs were in 3NT (one failing), twelve were in 1NT and four played in 2NT.

8. Dealer South : Game all

```
              ♠ K J 10 7 5 4
              ♡ A 5
              ◇ K 8
              ♣ A K 4
♠ Q 9 8 6        N         ♠ 3
♡ 9 8 4       W     E      ♡ 7 6
◇ A 7 3                    ◇ J 10 9 6 5 2
♣ Q 9 6          S         ♣ J 10 5 3
              ♠ A 2
              ♡ K Q J 10 3 2
              ◇ Q 4
              ♣ 8 7 2
```

West	North	East	South
			1♡
No	1♠	No	2♡
No	3♣	No	4♡
No	4NT	No	5♠ (1)
No	6♡	All pass	

(1) Two key cards for hearts plus the ♡Q

Source: 2005 World Championships, Round 17. North's 3♣
is a strong bid, virtually game-forcing since partner's rebid
might be 3NT. South's 4♡ shows a self-sufficient suit and
that re-assures North to look for slam. This is a good test to
decide whether a suit is self-sufficient: add the number of
honours in the long suit to the number of cards in that suit. If
the total is ten or more, treat the suit as self-sufficient.

38 of the 66 N-S pairs found 6♡ (3 failing), 13 played game
in hearts, six failed in 6♠ and six made game in spades.

9. Dealer West : N-S vulnerable

West	North	East	South
No	1♣	1♦	1♠
2♦	3♣	No	?

(Solution on page 69)

What would you do now as South with:

♠ K Q 9 6 3
♡ A 10 4
♦ K 5 4
♣ 8 5

10. Dealer North : Game all

West	North	East	South
	No	No	1♡
No	2♦	No	?

(Solution on page 70)

What would you do as South with:

♠ J
♡ A K Q 3 2
♦ A J 6 4 3
♣ A 7

11. Dealer West : Game all

West	North	East	South
2♦ (1)	No	?	

(1) Multi, weak two in hearts or in spades

(Solution on page 71)

What would you do as East with:

♠ 10 2
♡ 6 5 3
♦ A 10 5 3
♣ Q 9 8 7

12. Dealer South : E-W vulnerable

West	North	East	South
			No
1♡	Dble	No	2♡
Dble	3♣	3♡	?

(Solution on page 72)

What should South do with:

♠ J 10 5 4
♡ A 6 5
♦ K J 10 9 2
♣ J

9.   Dealer West : North-South vulnerable

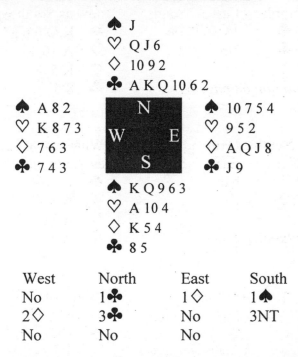

♠ J
♡ Q J 6
◇ 10 9 2
♣ A K Q 10 6 2

♠ A 8 2
♡ K 8 7 3
◇ 7 6 3
♣ 7 4 3

♠ 10 7 5 4
♡ 9 5 2
◇ A Q J 8
♣ J 9

♠ K Q 9 6 3
♡ A 10 4
◇ K 5 4
♣ 8 5

West	North	East	South
No	1♣	1◇	1♠
2◇	3♣	No	3NT
No	No	No	

Source: 2005 World Championships, Round 18. To be a winner requires courage. You need to be bold without being reckless. South's 3NT is a sensible risk, as North's 3♣ should show a strong suit and a respectable hand. If playing support doubles, North's failure to double 2◇ denies three spades and so South should not rebid the spades. To bid 3◇ to ask for a diamond stopper is unrealistic and will see North bidding 4♣. Now you have missed a decent 3NT. North's length in diamonds is a surprise, but that makes the play in 3NT much easier.

55 of the 66 pairs played in 3NT with 49 successful. Four failed in 5♣, two failed in 4♠ and three made 4♣.

10.   Dealer North : Game all

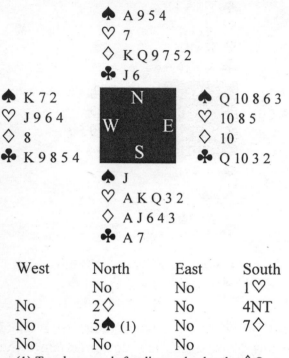

```
                      ♠ A 9 5 4
                      ♡ 7
                      ◇ K Q 9 7 5 2
                      ♣ J 6
  ♠ K 7 2           ┌─────────┐        ♠ Q 10 8 6 3
  ♡ J 9 6 4         │    N    │        ♡ 10 8 5
  ◇ 8               │ W     E │        ◇ 10
  ♣ K 9 8 5 4       │    S    │        ♣ Q 10 3 2
                    └─────────┘
                      ♠ J
                      ♡ A K Q 3 2
                      ◇ A J 6 4 3
                      ♣ A 7
```

West	North	East	South
	No	No	1♡
No	2◇	No	4NT
No	5♠ (1)	No	7◇
No	No	No	

(1) Two keys cards for diamonds plus the ◇Q.

Source: 2005 World Championships, Round 18. The excellent grand slam in diamonds should be reached whether North opens or not. It is easier, of course, if North does open 1◇. (1◇ : 1♡, 1♠ : 2♣ fourth-suit, 2◇ : 4NT, 5♠ : 7◇.) After No : 1♡, 2◇ it is foolish and lazy to jump to 6◇ when 4NT makes 7◇ a strong bet, since North's 2◇ by a passed hand figures to be a 5+ suit. At some tables 7◇ was reached after it began No : 1♡, 1♠ : 2◇ : 4◇ ...

48 of the 66 pairs made 7◇, 16 played in 6◇, while one was in 5◇ and one was in 4NT.

11.   Dealer West : Game all

<pre>
                    ♠ 8 6 5 4
                    ♥ K
                    ◇ K Q 2
                    ♣ K J 10 6 4·
    ♠ Q J   N   ♠ 10 2
    ♥ A Q 9 8 7 2   ♥ 6 5 3
    ◇ 8 7 4   W   E   ◇ A 10 5 3
    ♣ 5 2   S   ♣ Q 9 8 7
                    ♠ A K 9 7 3
                    ♥ J 10 4
                    ◇ J 9 6
                    ♣ A 3
</pre>

West	North	East	South
2◇	No	3♥ (1)	...

(1) Pass or correct

Source: 2005 World Championships, Round 19. It should be clear to East that North-South are almost certain to have a game somewhere and are very likely to have a fit in one of the majors. There is no safety in the jump to 3♥, asking partner to pass with hearts or bid 3♠ with spades, but it puts maximum pressure on N-S. This auction did not suffice:

West	North	East	South
2◇	No	2♥	No
No	Dble	No	4♠
No	No	No	

Perhaps 3♥ will not do either, but you must give it a try.

56 of the 66 N-S pairs played in 4♠. Five intrepid East-West pairs played in 3♥ undoubled, –400 x 3 and –300 x 2.

12.   Dealer South : East-West vulnerable

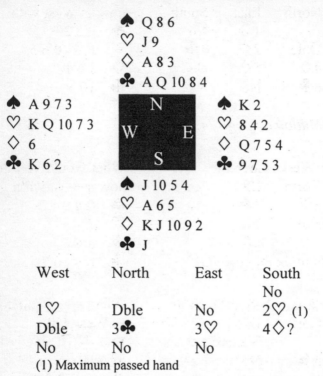

♠ Q 8 6
♡ J 9
◇ A 8 3
♣ A Q 10 8 4

♠ A 9 7 3
♡ K Q 10 7 3
◇ 6
♣ K 6 2

♠ K 2
♡ 8 4 2
◇ Q 7 5 4
♣ 9 7 5 3

♠ J 10 5 4
♡ A 6 5
◇ K J 10 9 2
♣ J

West	North	East	South
			No
1♡	Dble	No	2♡ (1)
Dble	3♣	3♡	4◇?
No	No	No	

(1) Maximum passed hand

Source: 2005 World Championships, Round 20. There are two important principles of competitive bidding here. (1) Do not compete a part-score to the 4-level unless you have excellent shape and prospects for game in the minor. (2) Do not bid the same values twice. South had said it all with 2♡ and so South should pass 3♡. That will end the auction and 3♡ will be at least one down instead of 4◇ going one down. The favourable vulnerability was no excuse for South bidding to the 4-level. It is essential that you know when to pass, not just when to bid. There was a great variation of scores from 3NT N-S making to 3NT, 4♣, 4♠ and 5◇ all three down.

13. Dealer East : N-S vulnerable

West	North	East	South
		1◇	No
1♡	Dble	2◇	3♣
3◇	4◇	5◇	No
No	6♣	No	No
?			

What would you do now as West with:

♠ 9 5 2
♡ K J 10 6 5
◇ J 6 4
♣ 10 5

(Solution on page 74)

14. Dealer West : Love all

West	North	East	South
1♠	2♡	4♠	5◇
No	No	?	

What would you do now as East with:

♠ Q J 9 5 3
♡ 7
◇ 6 5 2
♣ K J 10 7

(Solution on page 75)

15. Dealer East : N-S vulnerable

West	North	East	South
		No	1♠
4NT (1)	5♠	No	No
?			

(1) Freakish hand with both minors

What would you do as West with:

♠ ---
♡ 10 6
◇ A Q 9 8 3
♣ K J 6 5 4 3

(Solution on page 76)

16. Dealer South : N-S vulnerable

West	North	East	South
			1♣
Dble (1)	1◇	2♠	3♣
No	?		

(1) Alerted as 5-5 majors

What would you do next as North with:

♠ 6 5 3 2
♡ K 7
◇ 6 5 3 2
♣ A 10 4

(Solution on page 77)

13.   Dealer East : North-South vulnerable

                    ♠ A K Q 4
                    ♡ 8 7 2
                    ◇ 7
                    ♣ A K 9 7 2

♠ 9 5 2   **N**   ♠ 10 8 6
♡ K J 10 6 5   ♡ 4
◇ J 6 4   **W**   **E**   ◇ A K Q 10 9 8 2
♣ 10 5   **S**   ♣ J 8

                    ♠ J 7 3
                    ♡ A Q 9 3
                    ◇ 5 3
                    ♣ Q 6 4 3

West	North	East	South
		1◇	No
1♡	Dble	2◇	3♣
3◇	4◇	5◇	No
No	6♣	No	No
6◇	Dble	All pass	

Source: 2006 Pacific Asian Bridge Championships, Round 5. At most tables East started with a pre-empt in diamonds. At nine tables North doubled for takeout and South perished in some number of hearts. There is a greater temptation than usual to take a sacrifice at favourable vulnerability, but here West should have left North-South in 6♣ for a number of reasons. (1) Do not take a sacrifice if the opponents have been pressured into bidding a slam. (2) Do not take a sacrifice with a balanced hand. The cost is usually too high. (3) Do not bid the same values twice. West had done more than enough with the 3◇ bid. All further decisions belonged to East.

14.   Dealer West : Love all

```
                    ♠ 7
                    ♡ A 10 9 8 6 3
                    ◇ K
                    ♣ A Q 5 4 2
  ♠ A K 10 6 2          N          ♠ Q J 9 5 3
  ♡ Q J 4 2        W       E       ♡ 7
  ◇ J 3                            ◇ 6 5 2
  ♣ 9 3                S           ♣ K J 10 7
                    ♠ 8 4
                    ♡ K 5
                    ◇ A Q 10 9 8 7 4
                    ♣ 8 6
```

West	North	East	South
1♠	2♡	4♠	5◇
No	No	5♠?	No
No	Dble	All pass	

Source: 2006 Rosenblum World Open Teams, Round 1. East was out of line in bidding 5♠. East should have passed. This is another example where having bid your values you should leave the decision to partner. East's 4♠ described a weakish, unbalanced hand with good spade support. West decided against bidding 5♠ and East should respect that. East cannot tell whether 5◇ will succeed or whether 5♠ will prove too expensive. Either way East has no business bidding further. West can defeat 5◇ after the ♠A lead by switching to a trump. In practice 5♠ doubled went two down for –300.

Many pairs were failing in 4♠ and 5♡. There were 47 in 5◇, of which 18 were successful and 29 were defeated.

15.   Dealer East : North-South vulnerable

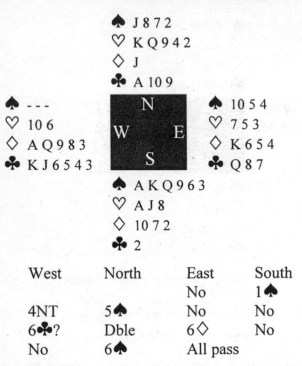

	♠ J 8 7 2		
	♡ K Q 9 4 2		
	♢ J		
	♣ A 10 9		

♠ - - -   ♠ 10 5 4
♡ 10 6   ♡ 7 5 3
♢ A Q 9 8 3   ♢ K 6 5 4
♣ K J 6 5 4 3   ♣ Q 8 7

♠ A K Q 9 6 3
♡ A J 8
♢ 10 7 2
♣ 2

West	North	East	South
		No	1♠
4NT	5♠	No	No
6♣?	Dble	6♢	No
No	6♠	All pass	

Source: Bridge Base Online in 2007. Here is another example where having shown your values you should not take further action. Notwithstanding the vulnerability West should pass 5♠. Partner has heard your 4NT and did not bid. Partner can also see the vulnerability and has not bid. You should abide by partner's decision to pass. It is true that 6♢ might not have cost much if South starts with a top spade, but another danger lurks behind bidding further. You push the opponents into an unbeatable slam. So it proved here as 6♠ made comfortably. East-West could have sacrificed again in 7♢, which can be defeated by five tricks on a club lead. How much better to have left South in 5♠.

16.   Dealer South : North-South vulnerable

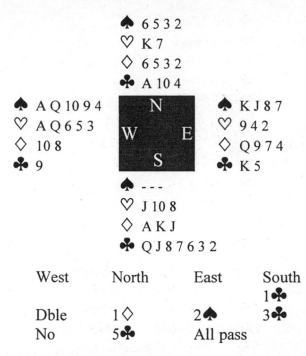

♠ 6 5 3 2
♥ K 7
♦ 6 5 3 2
♣ A 10 4

♠ A Q 10 9 4
♥ A Q 6 5 3
♦ 10 8
♣ 9

♠ K J 8 7
♥ 9 4 2
♦ Q 9 7 4
♣ K 5

♠ - - -
♥ J 10 8
♦ A K J
♣ Q J 8 7 6 3 2

West	North	East	South
			1♣
Dble	1♦	2♠	3♣
No	5♣	All pass	

Source: 2007 Zonal Teams Championship, Round 1. Even though the 1♣ opening was not artificial or forcing, West used the double to show the 5-5 pattern. This might not be the best use for a takeout double, but you need to be prepared for all eventualities. In long teams matches you and your partner will have prepared yourselves by being familiar with the bidding and carding methods of your opponents.

The evidence of the auction persuaded North to jump to 5♣. South would have a decent, long suit and was sure to be short in spades. In addition the ♥K looked to be well-placed. 5♣ was reached at two tables, with other contracts being 4♣ making five once and 4♠ failing at six tables.

17. Dealer East : N-S vulnerable

West	North	East	South
		1◇	2♣
2◇	3♣	3◇	3♠
No	?		

(Solution on page 79)

What would you do now as North with:

♠ A Q 8
♡ K 9 2
◇ 9 6 5
♣ 7 4 3 2

18. Dealer West : E-W vulnerable

West	North	East	South
No	No	No	?

(Solution on page 80)

How would you plan the bidding as South with:

♠ A 9
♡ A K 9 2
◇ A J
♣ A J 6 5 3

19. Dealer East : N-S vulnerable

West	North	East	South
		No	1♣ (1)
4♠	4NT (2)	No	5◇
No	6♣	No	6◇
No	No	?	

(1) Artificial, 16+ points
(2) General slam try

(Solution on page 81)

What would you do as East with:

♠ 10 7
♡ 9 6 4
◇ J 10 9 4
♣ A 10 5 3

20. Dealer West : E-W vulnerable

West	North	East	South
No	1◇	4♡	?

(Solution on page 82)

What would you do as South with:

♠ A 9 8 5 4
♡ 9
◇ K 10 9 8 4
♣ J 2

17.   Dealer East : North-South vulnerable

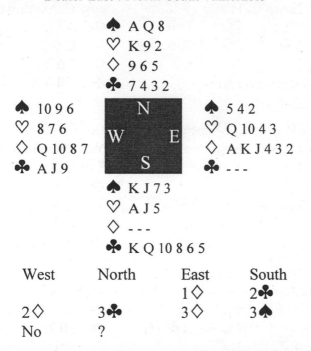

	♠ A Q 8	
	♡ K 9 2	
	◇ 9 6 5	
	♣ 7 4 3 2	

♠ 10 9 6   ♠ 5 4 2
♡ 8 7 6   ♡ Q 10 4 3
◇ Q 10 8 7   ◇ A K J 4 3 2
♣ A J 9   ♣ - - -

♠ K J 7 3
♡ A J 5
◇ - - -
♣ K Q 10 8 6 5

West	North	East	South
		1◇	2♣
2◇	3♣	3◇	3♠
No	?		

Source: 2007 Zonal Teams Championship. South's 3♠ is a try for game. South is exploring a possible 4-4 spade fit. Despite the flat shape, North could hardly be better, with four trumps and superb values in the majors. When faced with this situation two Norths jumped to 5♣, which was passed out. On seeing dummy South felt 6♣ was possible. The lucky/unlucky break in clubs meant that 5♣ was the limit. Single dummy you would want to be in 6♣. After 3♠ North might show a strong hand via a cue-bid of 4♡ or a jump to 4NT, not asking but showing a marvellous 5♣ raise, improved by the 3♠ bid. No pair reached 6♣, but two were in 5♣, four in 5♣ doubled, two in 5◇ doubled and one pair played in 4♠.

18.   Dealer West : East-West vulnerable

```
                    ♠ 7 6 3 2
                    ♡ 5 4
                    ◇ 9 7 6 2
                    ♣ K 10 7
   ♠ K Q 8 5 4          N           ♠ J 10
   ♡ 10 3                            ♡ Q J 8 7 6
   ◇ Q 5 4 3        W       E        ◇ K 10 8
   ♣ 9 4                S            ♣ Q 8 2
                    ♠ A 9
                    ♡ A K 9 2
                    ◇ A J
                    ♣ A J 6 5 3
```

This was a common auction:

West	North	East	South
No	No	No	2NT (1)
No	No	No	

(1) 20-22 balanced

Source: 2007 Zonal Teams Championship. Some Norths bid
on to game via 3♣ Stayman and finished in 3NT. With 3
HCP and no 5+ suit, it is usually best not to head for game if
a combined total of 25 points is the best possible. 3NT is
reasonable, but not marvellous since it depends on bringing
in the club suit. It would certainly be reasonable to be in 3NT
at teams vulnerable. The issue is about the valuation of the
South cards. To your 21 HCP you should add one for four
aces and one for the 5-card suit. That brings it to 23 points and
so open 2♣ and rebid 2NT to show 23-24 balanced. There
were five pairs in 2NT and three in 3NT, of whom one failed
by finessing the clubs into the East hand.

19.   Dealer East : North-South vulnerable

```
                    ♠ A 6
                    ♡ A 7 2
                    ◇ 5 3 2
                    ♣ K Q J 7 6
♠ Q J 9 8 5 4 3 2        N            ♠ 10 7
♡ 10 8 3                          ♡ 9 6 4
◇ - - -          W         E      ◇ J 10 9 4
♣ 8 4                S            ♣ A 10 5 3
                    ♠ K
                    ♡ K Q J 5
                    ◇ A K Q 8 7 6
                    ♣ 9 2
```

West	North	East	South
		No	1♣ (1)
4♠	4NT (2)	No	5◇
No	6♣	No	6◇
No	No	No	

(1) Artificial, 16+ points   (2) General slam try

Source: 2007 Zonal Teams Championship. East can be confident of beating 6◇, but must not double. At one table East doubled 6◇. On the spade lead, declarer can take the ♠A and play diamonds three times through East to deny East a trump trick. Another East doubled 6◇ and North ran to 6NT. East led the ♠10, won by the ♠K, and a club at trick 2 went to the king and ace. North won the heart exit, cashed the ♠A and then played the heart winners. The last heart squeezed East and 6NT was made. At another table it went 1◇ : (4♠) : 5♣ : (Double), 5◇ : (No) : No : (Double). All of these doubles are madness. West has not promised any defence.

20.   Dealer West : East-West vulnerable

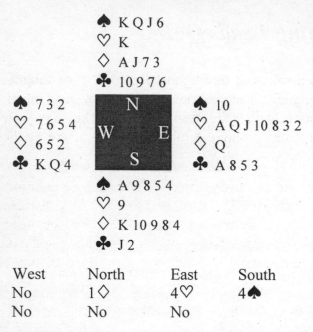

♠ K Q J 6
♡ K
◇ A J 7 3
♣ 10 9 7 6

♠ 7 3 2
♡ 7 6 5 4
◇ 6 5 2
♣ K Q 4

♠ 10
♡ A Q J 10 8 3 2
◇ Q
♣ A 8 5 3

♠ A 9 8 5 4
♡ 9
◇ K 10 9 8 4
♣ J 2

West	North	East	South
No	1◇	4♡	4♠
No	No	No	

Source: Finals of 2007 Zonal Teams Championship. At two of the four tables South bid 4♠. There is no safety in bidding 4♠, but if you are looking for safety, bridge is the wrong game for you. Bidding 4♠ is an acceptable risk in trying to be in game at the 4-level rather than at the 5-level. If 4♠ is doubled, you can then decide whether to run to 5◇. As it happens, there is no defence to 4♠.

At another table South bid 5◇ over 4♡. That would be defeated on the ♡A or ♣A lead, but makes on a spade or a diamond lead. At the last table South doubled 4♡, intending it for takeout, but North passed for penalties. It is vital that your partnership is confident of the meaning of such doubles. There are eleven tricks in hearts and 5♡ doubled was +990.

Chapter 7

Opening Leads Quiz

It is often said that finding the best lead is the toughest part of the game. Once dummy appears you have much more information at your disposal, but when choosing your lead, only your cards and the information from the auction are available to you.

You are said to have a blind lead when the auction is least helpful, such as 1NT : 3NT or 1♠ : 4♠, and the like. The more bidding, the more clues there are for your lead. It is vital that you stay focussed during the bidding and gauge the strength and shape of the opponents' hands from their bids.

It has been said that a top player could win any tournament if allowed to see dummy before the opening lead. Your task therefore is to estimate the likely contents of dummy. If you are not certain of the meaning of the opposition's bidding, make sure you ask them to explain the auction.

No doubt you already know many of the basic principles for the opening lead. Generally prefer to lead partner's suit and avoid suits bid by the opponents. In a trump contract it is not normally attractive to lead a suit headed by an ace unless the suit contains the ace and the king.

Unless dummy has shown a long suit, it is often better to make a passive lead from a suit with no honour cards than from a suit with one or two honours. When dummy has shown a long, useful suit, then you will do best to make an attacking lead (not a trump and not dummy's bid suit).

1. Dealer East : Game all

West	North	East	South
		No	3♠
No	4♣ (1)	No	4◇ (1)
No	4♡ (1)	No	5♣ (1)
No	6♠	All pass	

(1) Cue-bids, first- or second-round controls, with spades agreed as trumps

What would you lead as West with:

♠ 10 4
♡ 7 6 5
◇ A J 10
♣ A 9 5 4 3

(Solution on page 85)

2. Dealer South : E-W vulnerable

West	North	East	South
			No
2♠	Dble	No	3NT
No	No	No	

What would you lead as West with:

♠ K J 10 5 3 2
♡ Q 3
◇ J 2
♣ 6 4 2

(Solution on page 86)

3. Dealer South : Love all

West	North	East	South
			1♣ (1)
No	1◇ (2)	2♣	2NT (3)
No	3♡ (4)	No	3♠
No	No	No	

(1) Artificial, forcing 11+ points
(2) Artificial, negative, 0-9 points
(3) 18-20 balanced
(4) Transfer to spades

What would you lead as West with:

♠ 4 3
♡ A 9 7
◇ J 10 9 6 5 3
♣ 7 3

(Solution on page 87)

1. Dealer East : Game all

```
          ♠ K Q 8 2
          ♡ A Q 9 3
          ◇ K 9 8 6 5
          ♣ - - -
♠ 10 4         N         ♠ - - -
♡ 7 6 5                  ♡ K 10 8
◇ A J 10    W       E    ◇ Q 7 4 3
♣ A 9 5 4 3     S        ♣ Q J 10 7 6 2
          ♠ A J 9 7 6 5 3
          ♡ J 4 2
          ◇ 2
          ♣ K 8
```

West	North	East	South
		No	3♠
No	4♣ (1)	No	4◇ (1)
No	4♡ (1)	No	5♣ (1)
No	6♠	All pass	

(1) Cue-bids, first- or second-round controls, with spades agreed

Source: European Open Teams. Once South showed control in diamonds, why did North not bid 4NT? Because one of North's controls was a void, which had to be in clubs. After West led the ◇A, the switch to hearts was too late. Declarer rose with the ♡A, ruffed a diamond high, crossed to the ♠K and ruffed another low diamond high. A spade to the queen drew the last trump and declarer could discard two hearts on the ◇K and ◇9. At the other table after a similar auction (3♠ : 4♣, 4♠ : 5◇, 6♠) West found the vital heart lead. Declarer had to finesse. East won and returned a diamond.

2.   Dealer South : East-West vulnerable

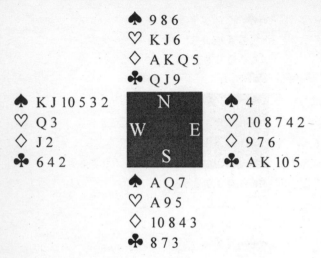

                    ♠ 9 8 6
                    ♡ K J 6
                    ◇ A K Q 5
                    ♣ Q J 9

♠ K J 10 5 3 2   N   ♠ 4
♡ Q 3   ♡ 10 8 7 4 2
◇ J 2   W   E   ◇ 9 7 6
♣ 6 4 2   ♣ A K 10 5
                            S
                    ♠ A Q 7
                    ♡ A 9 5
                    ◇ 10 8 4 3
                    ♣ 8 7 3

Source: 2005 Bermuda Bowl, Round 2. There were 22 tables
in play and 3NT was reached twenty times, ten times with
North declarer and ten times by South.

After 2♠ by West, double from North and 3NT by South, it
is highly likely that a spade lead will give away a trick. East
has not shown support for spades and South, a passed hand,
has jumped to 3NT. It is a very strong chance that South
holds ♠A-Q.

Three Wests did lead a spade, giving South the ninth trick.
Three led a heart and each South failed, even though they
could have succeeded: cash ♠A, play off the red suits and
endplay East with a club to the queen. Four Wests judged
that a spade lead would give a trick away and as both red
suits looked too risky, they chose a club. After East captures
dummy's club honour and returns a spade, there is no way
for declarer to succeed.

3.   Dealer South : Love all

               ♠ Q J 7 6 5 2
               ♡ 6 4
               ♢ 7 2
               ♣ 10 6 4

West		East
♠ 4 3		♠ 9 8
♡ A 9 7		♡ K J 3 2
♢ J 10 9 6 5 3		♢ A 8
♣ 7 3		♣ K Q J 5 2

               ♠ A K 10
               ♡ Q 10 8 5
               ♢ K Q 4
               ♣ A 9 8

West	North	East	South
			1♣ (1)
No	1♢ (2)	2♣	2NT (3)
No	3♡ (4)	No	3♠
No	No	No	

(1) Artificial, forcing 11+ points
(2) Artificial, negative, 0-9 points
(3) 18-20 balanced
(4) Transfer to spades

Source: 2005 World Championships, Round 14. Partner has made an overcall at the 2-level. This indicates a respectable hand and a decent suit. You need a very strong reason to choose something other than partner's suit. Start with a club and 3♠ will be defeated. Try to be clever and lead the ♢J and declarer makes 3♠. The normal lead is usually best.

Out of 66 pairs, 16 played in 3♠ and 11 were defeated. 23 pairs were much too high in 4♠ and none succeeded.

4. Dealer North : Love all

West	North	East	South
	2◇ (1)	No	2♡ (2)
No	No	Dble	No
3◇	3♡	All pass	

(1) Multi, weak two in hearts or spades
(2) Pass with hearts, correct with spades

(Solution on page 89)

What would you lead as West with:

♠ K 2
♡ Q 8 4
◇ Q 10 9 7 6
♣ 8 7 2

5. Dealer South : Love all

West	North	East	South
			1♠
No	2♣	2♡	2♠
4♡	6♣	Dble	6♠
No	No	Dble	All pass

(Solution on page 90)

Playing pairs, what would you lead as West with:

♠ 9 7 6 3
♡ K 10 9 7 4
◇ J 10 5
♣ 3

6. Dealer West : Love all

West	North	East	South
1♠	3♣ (1)	No	4♡
No	4♠ (2)	No	6♡
No	No	No	

(1) Two-suiter, hearts and diamonds
(2) Cue-bid, hearts agreed as trumps

(Solution on page 91)

Playing pairs, what would you lead as West with:

♠ Q 9 8 7 6 5
♡ 10 2
◇ A K 7 5
♣ 9

7. Dealer West : Game all

West	North	East	South
No	2♡ (1)	No	2♠
No	3♡	No	3♠
No	No	No	

(1) Weak two in hearts

(Solution on page 92)

What would you lead as West with:

♠ A J 3 2
♡ 2
◇ 10 9 8
♣ Q 10 8 5 4

4. Dealer North : Love all

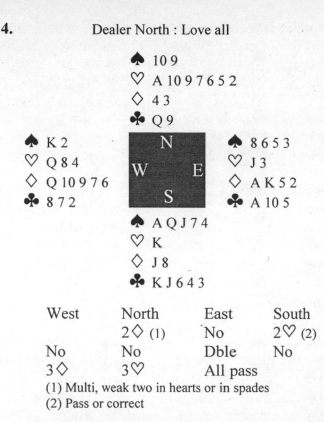

	♠ 10 9		
	♡ A 10 9 7 6 5 2		
	◇ 4 3		
	♣ Q 9		
♠ K 2			♠ 8 6 5 3
♡ Q 8 4			♡ J 3
◇ Q 10 9 7 6			◇ A K 5 2
♣ 8 7 2			♣ A 10 5
	♠ A Q J 7 4		
	♡ K		
	◇ J 8		
	♣ K J 6 4 3		

West	North	East	South
	2◇ (1)	No	2♡ (2)
No	No	Dble	No
3◇	3♡	All pass	

(1) Multi, weak two in hearts or in spades
(2) Pass or correct

Source: 2005 World Championships, Round 16. It is tempting to start with the ♠K. You hope partner has the ♠A and can give you a spade ruff. Alas, the ♠K lets declarer succeed.

There is no need for heroics with the spade lead. Make the normal lead of the ◇10 and you will beat 3♡. East wins and can shift to the spade. You collect one spade, one heart, two diamonds and a club. Why should you reject the spade lead? North's undisciplined 3♡ bid suggests seven hearts and so North is unlikely to hold three spades. You have a potential trump trick anyway and the ruff will not give you more tricks.

5.   Dealer South : Love all

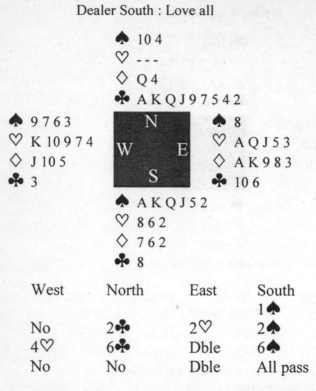

♠ 10 4
♡ - - -
◇ Q 4
♣ A K Q J 9 7 5 4 2

♠ 9 7 6 3
♡ K 10 9 7 4
◇ J 10 5
♣ 3

♠ 8
♡ A Q J 5 3
◇ A K 9 8 3
♣ 10 6

♠ A K Q J 5 2
♡ 8 6 2
◇ 7 6 2
♣ 8

West	North	East	South
			1♠
No	2♣	2♡	2♠
4♡	6♣	Dble	6♠
No	No	Dble	All pass

Source: 2006 World Open Pairs, Qualifying Round 2. The jump to 6♣ by North without using 4NT indicates a void, surely in hearts. If East has winners in clubs they can hardly vanish. Likewise with any spade winners. East's second double definitely says, 'Do not lead a heart,' and hence you should start with the ◇J. That ensures the contract is at least one down. On a heart or a spade lead declarer has all thirteen tricks. 6♠ doubled, N-S 1310, was a shared top. Best E-W scores were 6♡ doubled making, followed by 6♠ doubled down five (twice), once on a club lead and once on a diamond lead and club switch.

6.   Dealer West : Love all

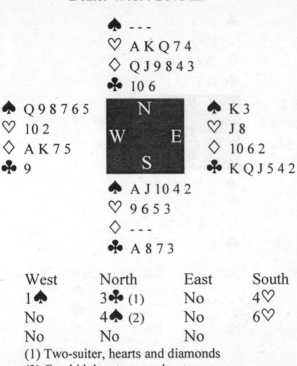

♠ - - -
♡ A K Q 7 4
◇ Q J 9 8 4 3
♣ 10 6

♠ Q 9 8 7 6 5   ♠ K 3
♡ 10 2   ♡ J 8
◇ A K 7 5   ◇ 10 6 2
♣ 9   ♣ K Q J 5 4 2

♠ A J 10 4 2
♡ 9 6 5 3
◇ - - -
♣ A 8 7 3

West	North	East	South
1♠	3♣ (1)	No	4♡
No	4♠ (2)	No	6♡
No	No	No	

(1) Two-suiter, hearts and diamonds
(2) Cue-bid, hearts agreed as trumps

Source: 2006 World Open Pairs, Qualifying Round 2. How can declarer avoid losing two diamonds? By ruffing the diamonds out. How can you reduce that possibility? By leading trumps. When dummy has shown two suits and declarer has chosen one, a trump lead is often best to protect your winners in the other suit. If you start with the ◇K, declarer can make 6♡ easily. A trump lead or, as it happens, a low spade or a club lead will defeat the slam. 6♡ was bid 21 times and made eight times, with seven Wests leading a top diamond. It failed 13 times, but only once was a trump led.

7.   Dealer West : Game all

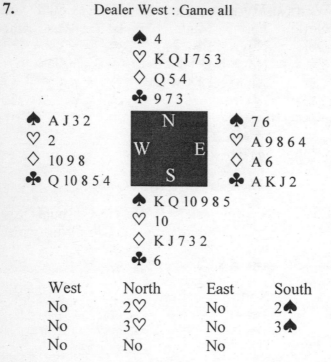

♠ 4
♡ K Q J 7 5 3
◇ Q 5 4
♣ 9 7 3

♠ A J 3 2
♡ 2
◇ 10 9 8
♣ Q 10 8 5 4

♠ 7 6
♡ A 9 8 6 4
◇ A 6
♣ A K J 2

♠ K Q 10 9 8 5
♡ 10
◇ K J 7 3 2
♣ 6

West	North	East	South
No	2♡	No	2♠
No	3♡	No	3♠
No	No	No	

Source: Final of a 2006 National Teams Championship. The bidding makes it clear that South has no tolerance for hearts. West has two trump tricks and has no intermediate trump to promote. That rules out a heart (although a heart lead works). There is a sound principle for an opening lead when you hold 4+ trumps: 'Trump length, lead length'. The idea is to force declarer to ruff and so shorten declarer's trump holding. Any lead can defeat 3♠ here, but the club lead (or heart lead and club switch) does most damage. In practice West led a club and South ruffed the second club. After ◇2 to the queen and ace, East returned a diamond, South won and played a third diamond, ruffed by East. Outcome: three down.

8. Dealer West : E-W vulnerable

West	North	East	South
1♦	Dble	No	2♣
No	3♠ (1)	No	4♡ (2)
No	4♠	All pass	

(1) Inviting game
(2) Choice of contracts

What would you lead as West with:

♠ A 5 3
♡ A J 5 2
♦ K 6 5 2
♣ 5 3

(Solution on page 94)

9. Dealer East : N-S vulnerable

West	North	East	South
		No	1♡
2♦	Dble	3♦	3♠
No	4♠	5♦	5♠
No	No	No	

What would you lead as West with:

♠ J 3
♡ 8
♦ A 10 9 6 5 3
♣ K J 8 3

(Solution on page 95)

10. Dealer South : N-S vulnerable

West	North	East	South
			1♡
No	2NT (1)	No	3♡ (2)
No	4♡	All pass	

(1) Artificial, game-forcing heart raise
(2) Minimum opening, no void, no singleton

What would you lead as West with:

♠ K 10 4 2
♡ J 4
♦ 9 7 4
♣ 10 9 4 3

(Solution on page 96)

8.   Dealer West : East-West vulnerable

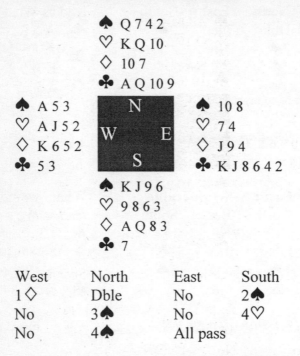

West	North	East	South
1◇	Dble	No	2♠
No	3♠	No	4♡
No	4♠	All pass	

Source: Final, 2007 Zonal Teams Championship. South's sequence is a little strange, but not everyone bids as well as you do (South might have bid 2◇ in reply to the double). With more spades than hearts, South would have bid 4♠ over 3♠. Offering 4♡ as a choice of games suggests South has equal length in the majors and North figures to have some length in hearts for the takeout double. If N-S have eight hearts together, ♡A and a heart gives East a ruff at once. If N-S have seven hearts, ♡A and another heart allows you to give East a heart ruff later. Without South's help you might have started with a diamond lead, after which South can succeed. On the actual deal a spade lead also works.

9.   Dealer East : North-South vulnerable

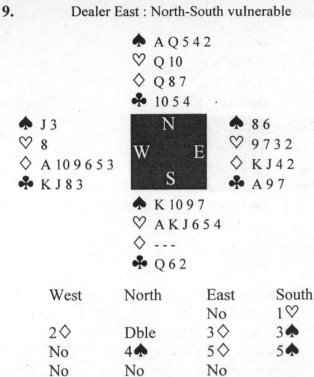

| ♠ A Q 5 4 2 |
| ♡ Q 10 |
| ♦ Q 8 7 |
| ♣ 10 5 4 |

♠ J 3   ♠ 8 6
♡ 8   ♡ 9 7 3 2
♦ A 10 9 6 5 3   ♦ K J 4 2
♣ K J 8 3   ♣ A 9 7

| ♠ K 10 9 7 |
| ♡ A K J 6 5 4 |
| ♦ - - - |
| ♣ Q 6 2 |

West	North	East	South
		No	1♡
2♦	Dble	3♦	3♠
No	4♣	5♦	5♠
No	No	No	

Source: Final, 2007 Zonal Team Championship. The deal was played at four tables. At two North played in 6♠ and both Easts began with the ♣A for two down, E-W +200. One North played in 5♠ on the ♦2 lead for +710. At the remaining table, after the given auction, West led the ♦A and South scored +710. On the bidding it is clear that the defence will not collect many tricks in diamonds. If East has any tricks in the majors they will not run away, but the most likely hope for tricks is the club suit. West should lead a low club before declarer can draw trumps and use the heart suit to discard losers from dummy.

10.   Dealer South : North-South vulnerable

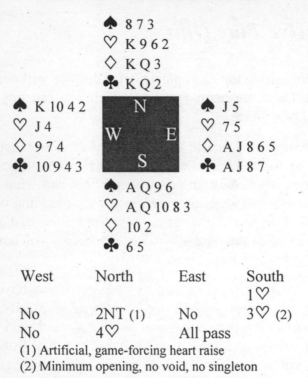

♠ 8 7 3
♡ K 9 6 2
◇ K Q 3
♣ K Q 2

♠ K 10 4 2
♡ J 4
◇ 9 7 4
♣ 10 9 4 3

♠ J 5
♡ 7 5
◇ A J 8 6 5
♣ A J 8 7

♠ A Q 9 6
♡ A Q 10 8 3
◇ 10 2
♣ 6 5

West	North	East	South
			1♡
No	2NT (1)	No	3♡ (2)
No	4♡	All pass	

(1) Artificial, game-forcing heart raise
(2) Minimum opening, no void, no singleton

Source: Final, 2007 National Teams Championship. Some bid 4♡ as South to show this hand type. Others use 3♣ over 2NT with any minimum. Both tables had effectively the same sequence. At one table West led a low spade and as a result declarer made 4♡ for +620. At the other West led the ◇7. East captured dummy's honour and shifted to a spade. Now South lost two spades, a club and a diamond for one down. When dummy has shown a useful long suit, an attacking lead is usually best. With no such evidence of a long suit in dummy, a passive lead is preferred. That suggests a diamond lead here, with a club as second choice.

Chapter 8

Defensive Play Quiz

If you want to be a top class player, your defence will need to be sharp. There are many ways in which you can improve your level of defence.

Good defence starts before the opening lead. You must pay attention to the bidding. Do not waft off just because you have a poor hand. Note the opponents' bids and what they indicate in terms of strength and shape. If their bidding began 1♠ : 1NT, 2♢ you already know declarer has at least a 5-4 pattern. The more they bid, the more information you have to help you to find the best defence.

What do you do as soon as dummy appears? If you have not been counting dummy's High Card Points automatically, it is time to start doing that, hand after hand. You add your own high card values to dummy's and subtract the total from 40. That tells you how many HCP are held between declarer and your partner. You can usually make an educated estimate of declarer's range of points and from that you deduce partner's possible strength. That might help you to avoid a futile line of defence. If partner's range of points is 3-5, it is no use playing partner for an ace and a king.

You must also note the card led by partner and what follows from that. You then gauge the tricks you have and where you might score any extra tricks. You have to decide whether to adopt an attacking defence (when dummy has a long, strong suit) or a passive defence. Partnership signalling is also of the utmost importance.

1.   ♠ Q 5
Dealer West   ♡ Q J 5 4
Love all   ◇ A J 9 7 5
                                      ♣ 10 5

♠ 7 6 4 3
♡ A
◇ K 10 4 3
♣ A K 8 4

West	North	East	South
1♠*	No	2♠	No
No	Dble	No	3♡
No	No	No	

West leads the ♣A, East plays the ♣9, discouraging, ♣3 from South. West shifts to the ♠7: five – ace – eight. East returns the ♣6: seven – king – 10.   (*Dictated by system)

What should West play at trick 4? (Solution on page 100)

2.   ♠ J 8 5 2
Dealer South   ♡ K
Love all   ◇ Q 9 8 6
                                      ♣ K J 8 6

♠ K 6
♡ J 6 5 3
◇ 10 4
♣ A 10 7 5 4

Playing 5-card majors, South opens 1♠, North raises to 3♠ and South bids 4♠. The early play:

1. West leads the ♡3: king – ace.

2. East returns the ♠7 and South wins with the ♠A.

3. ♣Q from South. You take ♣A, ♣2 from East (reverse count).

What do you play at trick 4? (Solution on page 101)

3.   ♠ 7 5 3
Dealer East   ♡ J 8 3
E-W vulnerable   ◇ K Q 7 5 3 2
                                          ♣ 8

```
              N              ♠ K 10
         W         E         ♡ Q 7 4
              S              ◇ A 8
                             ♣ A 10 9 4 3 2
```

West	North	East	South
		1♣	1♠
2◇ (1)	Dble (2)	2♡	3◇
No	No	No	

(1) Transfer to hearts   (2) Shows diamonds

1. West leads the ♣6 and you win with the ♣A.

What do you play at trick 2?(Solution on page 102)

4.   ♠ - - -
Dealer East   ♡ K Q J 8 5 4 2
Game all   ◇ A Q 8
                                          ♣ J 8 2

```
♠ Q 9 7 5        N
♡ A 9 6 3
◇ J 9 4     W         E
♣ A 9            S
```

West	North	East	South
		2NT (1)	4♠
Dble	No	No	No

(1) Weak, both minors

West leads the ♣A: two – ten – four. If partner is known to have a 5+ suit, odd cards = encouraging, even cards = suit-preference.

What do you play at trick 2? (Solution on page 103)

1.   Dealer West : Love all

```
                  ♠ Q 5
                  ♡ Q J 5 4
                  ◇ A J 9 7 5
                  ♣ 10 5
   ♠ 7 6 4 3         N           ♠ A 10 9 2
   ♡ A                           ♡ 10 9 8 6
   ◇ K 10 4 3     W     E        ◇ 8 2
   ♣ A K 8 4         S           ♣ 9 6 2
                  ♠ K J 8
                  ♡ K 7 3 2
                  ◇ Q 6
                  ♣ Q J 7 3
```

West	North	East	South
1♠ (1)	No	2♠	No
No	Dble	No	3♡
No	No	No	

(1) Dictated by system

Source: 2005 World Championships, Round 2. West led the
♣A and East played the discouraging ♣9. West shifted to
the ♠7, denying interest in spades. East returned the ♣6 to
the seven, king and ten. West had to decide how to continue.

East's ♠A had denied the ♠K and so there were no more
spade tricks for the defence. There was no way for declarer
to avoid a diamond loser and so a diamond switch was not
needed. As cashing the trump ace is pointless, West should
continue with a third club. South wins and plays a low
trump. West takes the ♡A perforce and now the fourth
round of clubs promotes a trump trick for East. One down.

2.   Dealer South : Love all

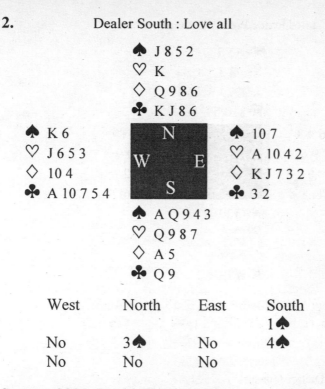

            ♠ J 8 5 2
            ♡ K
            ◇ Q 9 8 6
            ♣ K J 8 6

♠ K 6   ♠ 10 7
♡ J 6 5 3   ♡ A 10 4 2
◇ 10 4   ◇ K J 7 3 2
♣ A 10 7 5 4   ♣ 3 2

            ♠ A Q 9 4 3
            ♡ Q 9 8 7
            ◇ A 5
            ♣ Q 9

West	North	East	South
			1♠
No	3♠	No	4♠
No	No	No	

Source: 2005 World Championships, Round 13. West leads the ♡3 and East wins with the ace. The ♠7 return is taken by South with the ace and the ♣Q comes next. West wins with the ♣A, East playing the ♣2 (reverse count).

Since there are no more tricks for the defence in hearts or clubs, the obvious switch is to the ◇10. That will be enough to defeat 4♠. Indeed, without values in diamonds, East would have shifted to a diamond. Be careful, though. Do not cash the ♠K before switching to the ◇10. East needs the second spade to ruff the third round of clubs. On any card but a diamond at trick 4, 4♠ can succeed. 61 of 66 pairs were in 4♠. 28 made it and 33 were defeated.

3.   Dealer East : East-West vulnerable

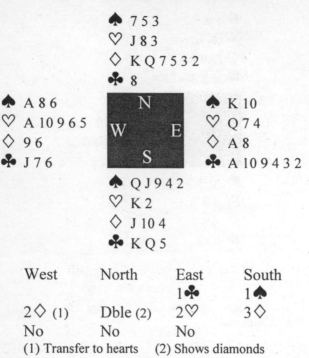

♠ 7 5 3
♡ J 8 3
◇ K Q 7 5 3 2
♣ 8

♠ A 8 6
♡ A 10 9 6 5
◇ 9 6
♣ J 7 6

♠ K 10
♡ Q 7 4
◇ A 8
♣ A 10 9 4 3 2

♠ Q J 9 4 2
♡ K 2
◇ J 10 4
♣ K Q 5

West	North	East	South
		1♣	1♠
2◇ (1)	Dble (2)	2♡	3◇
No	No	No	

(1) Transfer to hearts   (2) Shows diamonds

Source: 2005 World Championships, Round 16. The ♣6 lead went to the ace and East shifted to the ♡4. South played low and West won. South took the heart return and discarded two spades from dummy on the clubs. Thus, 3◇ made.

Why should East find the switch to the ♠K at trick 2 (to beat 3◇ by two tricks)? Ask yourself where are five tricks for the defence. There are no more club tricks and as West's club lead denies holding ♡A-K, you cannot expect more than one heart trick. If South's spades are headed by the A-Q, you can score only one spade trick and will not defeat 3◇. Therefore assume South's spades are worse and play the ♠K.

4.   Dealer East : Game all

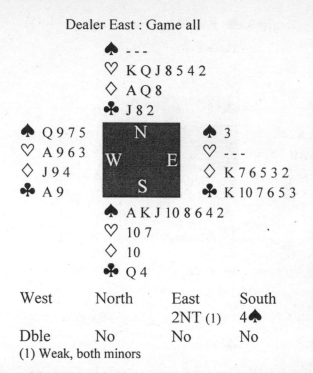

West	North	East	South
		2NT (1)	4♠
Dble	No	No	No

(1) Weak, both minors

Source: 2005 World Championships, Round 18. Some Easts opened 4NT rather than 2NT. 37 Wests played 5◇ doubled on the ♡K lead and 35 declarers made it for +750. Each of the four Easts in 5◇ doubled failed after the ♠A lead.

Against 4♠ doubled West starts with the ♣A and East's ♣10 is a suit-preference signal for a heart switch. (The ♣3 would request another club and the ♣6 would ask for a diamond shift.) As East is asking for a heart West should switch to the ♡A, followed by the ♡3 (asking for a club back). East ruffs the ♡3 and plays ♣K followed by a third club. If South discards or ruffs low, West ruffs cheaply. If South ruffs with the ♠J or ♠10, West discards and scores two trump tricks later. Either way East-West collect +800.

5.   ♠ 9 8 5 4
Dealer East   ♡ A 8 5
Game all   ◇ K 9 5
                                         ♣ A Q 6

```
              N              ♠ 7 3
                             ♡ 6 4
          W       E          ◇ A J 10 7 6 4
              S              ♣ K 4 2
```

West	North	East	South
		No	2♡ (1)
No	2NT (2)	No	3♡ (3)
No	No	No	

(1) Weak two   (2) Strong inquiry   (3) Minimum

West starts with ♠A, ♠K and ♠Q. South plays ♠2, ♠6, ♠10.

What should East play on the third spade? (Solution on page 106)

6.   ♠ Q 10 5
Dealer North   ♡ Q 9 3 2
Love all   ◇ K 5 4 3 2
                                         ♣ 10

```
♠ K 4         N
♡ A J 5
◇ 9 6     W       E
♣ J 7 6 5 3 2     S
```

South opens 1♠ and North raises to 2♠. South makes a trial bid of 3♡, seeking help in hearts, and North raises to 4♡. South reverts to 4♠.

West leads the ◇9: king – jack – seven. Declarer plays the ♠Q from dummy: two – three – king.

What should West play at trick 3? (Solution on page 107)

7.

Dealer North

E-W vulnerable

	♠ K 10
	♡ A J 8 6
	◇ A Q J 9 8
	♣ J 6

♠ 9	N
♡ K 10 4 3	
◇ 6 5 4 3	W E
♣ A K 5 4	S

West	North	East	South
	1◇	No	1♠
No	2♡	No	2♠
No	3♠	No	4♠
No	No	No	

West leads the ♣A.

How would you continue if East plays the:
(a) ♣9, discouraging? (b) ♣2, encouraging (c) ♣Q? *(see p.108)*

8.

Dealer South

Game all

	♠ 8 6 2	
	♡ Q J 10 9 8 7 4 2	
	◇ 2	
	♣ K	

N		♠ A Q J 10 5 3
		♡ - - -
W E		◇ 7 3
S		♣ J 9 8 5 3

West	North	East	South
			1◇
Dble	1♡	2♠	5◇
No	No	No	

West leads the ♡A. What should East play on that?

Plan East's defence. (Solution page 109)

5.   Dealer East : Game all

                          ♠ 9 8 5 4
                          ♡ A 8 5
                          ◇ K 9 5
                          ♣ A Q 6

♠ A K Q J   ♠ 7 3
♡ J 7   N   ♡ 6 4
◇ 8 3 2   W   E   ◇ A J 10 7 6 4
♣ 9 8 7 3   S   ♣ K 4 2

                          ♠ 10 6 2
                          ♡ K Q 10 9 3 2
                          ◇ Q
                          ♣ J 10 5

West	North	East	South
		No	2♡ (1)
No	2NT (2)	No	3♡ (3)
No	No	No	

(1) Weak two   (2) Strong inquiry   (3) Minimum

Source: Finals, 2005 Bermuda Bowl, Venice Cup, Board 26.
Each South began with a weak 2♡ or a multi-2◇. Each North
invited game despite the shape and modest point count. Three
played in 3♡, one in 4♡. With North declarer two Easts led a
spade (no need for an attacking club lead on this auction).
Both Wests produced a club switch in time to defeat declarer.
With South declarer one West led a top spade and shifted to a
club at trick 2. At the remaining table West began with the top
spades and East had to make a discard on the third spade. East
unwisely asked for a diamond switch instead of a club (the
◇ 4 as suit-preference for clubs would do). West led the ◇ 8:
nine – ten – queen and now the defence could not beat 3♡.

6. Dealer North : Love all

```
              ♠ Q 10 5
              ♡ Q 9 3 2
              ◇ K 5 4 3 2
              ♣ 10
♠ K 4          N          ♠ 9 2
♡ A J 5      W   E        ♡ K 8 4
◇ 9 6          S          ◇ J 10 8
♣ J 7 6 5 3 2            ♣ A Q 9 8 4
              ♠ A J 8 7 6 3
              ♡ 10 7 6
              ◇ A Q 7
              ♣ K
```

West	North	East	South
	No	No	1♠
No	2♠	No	3♡ (1)
No	4♡	No	4♠
No	No	No	

(1) Long suit trial bid

Source: 2006 Pacific Asian Teams Championship, Round 10. Seven N-S pairs played in a spade part-score, six were in 4♠, four making, and one E-W saved in 5♣ doubled for –300.

After the ◇9 lead taken by the king, East's ◇J denies the ◇Q and so declarer is known to hold ◇A, ◇Q. With no diamond tricks coming, you need to collect one club and two hearts, but the order is important. Cash the ♡A first and then continue with a club or the ♡J: queen – king. East will cash the ♣A before playing a third heart. At the table West erred and played a club at trick 3. East won and, thinking a diamond ruff was sought, returned a diamond for –420.

7.   Dealer North : East-West vulnerable

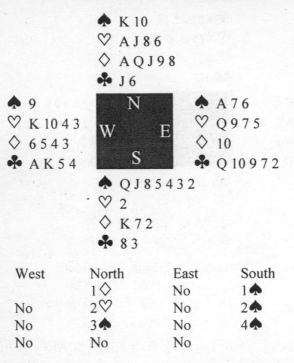

West	North	East	South
	1♦	No	1♠
No	2♥	No	2♠
No	3♠	No	4♠
No	No	No	

Source: 2006 Rosenblum, World Open Teams, Round 4. West leads a top club against 4♠. East wants a diamond ruff, but how to tell West? If East discourages clubs, the obvious switch is to hearts, not diamonds. If East encourages clubs, it makes sense only if East began with a doubleton club, which gives South five clubs, not likely. Dismiss that possibility and West might see the ♣2 as suit-preference for diamonds. Best is the ♣Q, an 'alarm clock signal' to do something very unusual. Now West should find the diamond shift. 4♠ was played 124 times and made 70 times. With North declarer, 64 times on the ♦10 lead, 4♠ was beaten 44 times. With South declarer, 4♠ was beaten only 10 times out of 60.

8.   Dealer South : Game all

```
                    ♠ 8 6 2
                    ♡ Q J 10 9 8 7 4 2
                    ◇ 2
                    ♣ K
   ♠ K 9 7 4          N          ♠ A Q J 10 5 3
   ♡ A K 6 5                     ♡ - - -
   ◇ K 6      W           E      ◇ 7 3
   ♣ 10 6 4          S          ♣ J 9 8 5 3
                    ♠ - - -
                    ♡ 3
                    ◇ A Q J 10 9 8 5 4
                    ♣ A Q 7 2
```

West	North	East	South
			1◇
Dble	1♡	2♠	5◇
No	No	No	

Source: 2007 Zonal Teams Championship. Most would opt for 4♠ by East, but that was the actual auction. West began with the ♡A. East played an encouraging spade and that was the end of the defence. South ruffed the spade at trick 2, crossed to the ♣K, ruffed a spade, ruffed a low club in dummy and lost only one heart and one diamond.

How hard is it for East to see the need to ruff the ♡A and return a trump? To choose the top heart lead rather than a spade, West's hearts must be headed by the A-K. For the takeout double West is likely to have four hearts. That means that dummy's hearts will be useless and the only other value in dummy is the ruffing potential. The trump switch puts paid to that at once. If a spade trick is coming, it can come later.

9.   ♠ 10 7 2
Dealer East   ♡ A K Q 8 6
N-S vulnerable   ♢ K 6
                                       ♣ 10 4 3

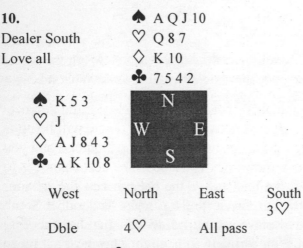

♠ 5 4
♡ 4 3
♢ A J 7 5 4 3 2
♣ K 9

West	North	East	South
		No	1♠
3♢ (1)	4♠	All pass	

(1) Weak jump-overcall

West starts with the ♢A: six – ten – eight.

What should West play at trick 2? (Solution on page 111)

10.   ♠ A Q J 10
Dealer South   ♡ Q 8 7
Love all   ♢ K 10
                                       ♣ 7 5 4 2

♠ K 5 3
♡ J
♢ A J 8 4 3
♣ A K 10 8

West	North	East	South
			3♡
Dble	4♡	All pass	

West leads the ♣A: two – nine (discouraging) – jack. West continues with the ♣K: four – six – queen.

What should West play at trick 3? (Solution on page 112)

9. Dealer East : North-South vulnerable

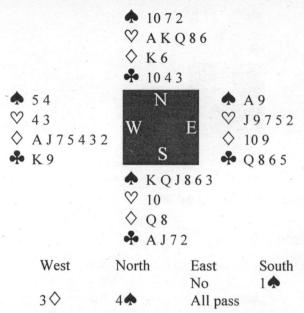

<pre>
               ♠ 10 7 2
               ♡ A K Q 8 6
               ◇ K 6
               ♣ 10 4 3
  ♠ 5 4   ♠ A 9
  ♡ 4 3   N   ♡ J 9 7 5 2
  ◇ A J 7 5 4 3 2   W   E   ◇ 10 9
  ♣ K 9   S   ♣ Q 8 6 5
               ♠ K Q J 8 6 3
               ♡ 10
               ◇ Q 8
               ♣ A J 7 2
</pre>

West	North	East	South
		No	1♠
3◇	4♠	All pass	

Source: 2007 Zonal Teams Championship. One might prefer
3♡ by North, followed by 4♠ over South's 3♠, but the actual
bidding was as above. West starts with the ◇A. What next?

This is simply a matter of finding four tricks for the defence.
The ◇A is one. Where are the other three? There will be none
from hearts. Even if East can ruff the second diamond and you
score the ♣K, one more trick is needed. The best chance is to
play East for the ♣A and shift to the ♣K at trick 2. East does
not have the ♣K, but East's holding is just as good. If South
takes the ♣A and plays a trump, East wins, cashes the ♣Q
and gives West a club ruff. South might play hearts first to
discard two clubs, but as the cards lie, this does not work. At
six tables where South played game in spades, every West led
the ◇A, but only three shifted to the ♣K to beat the contract.

10.   Dealer South : Love all

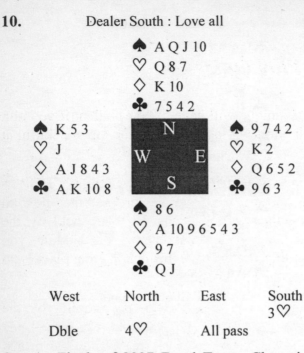

           ♠ A Q J 10
           ♡ Q 8 7
           ◇ K 10
           ♣ 7 5 4 2

♠ K 5 3   ♠ 9 7 4 2
♡ J   ♡ K 2
◇ A J 8 4 3   ◇ Q 6 5 2
♣ A K 10 8   ♣ 9 6 3

           ♠ 8 6
           ♡ A 10 9 6 5 4 3
           ◇ 9 7
           ♣ Q J

West	North	East	South
			3♡
Dble	4♡	All pass	

Source: Finals of 2007 Zonal Teams Championship. At two tables East played a spade part-score after South opened a weak 2♡ or a multi-2◇. At the other two tables the auction went as above. One West started with ♣A, ◇A, ♣K and a third club, ruffed. Declarer played for the best chance and laid down the ♡A. One down.

The other West started with the ♣A, ♣K, but then foolishly played a third club, a futile defence. West can see there are no spade tricks for the defence and no more than two club tricks. West should cash the ◇A and hope East has a trump trick. After ruffing the club at trick 3 declarer took a spade finesse, came to hand with a heart to the ace and finessed in spades again. When the ♠A felled the ♠K, both of declarer's diamond losers vanished.

Chapter 9

Declarer Play Quiz

Your declarer technique will have to be excellent if you aim to be a frequent winner. Most players at the top are skilful at declarer play.

Just as in defence, you start by counting dummy's HCP as soon as dummy appears. Add your own and subtract the total from 40. That tells you how many HCP are held by the opponents. If either opponent has been in the bidding, you can estimate the likely range of points held by that player and hence the rest for the other opponent.

Naturally you pay close attention to any bidding by the opposition. Even if they have not bid, there can be tell-tale clues. If a player who could not open the bidding has turned up with 9-10 HCP, do not expect them to hold any more. It is even easier against those who play light-opening systems, 10-14 or similar, and fail to open. If they turn up with 7-8 HCP and have not opened, you can usually place the missing high cards with their partner.

Make sure you know the leading and signalling methods of the opponents. There are many inferences from the lead and the play by third hand. You can read the opponents' suit lengths very accurately if they play rigorous count signals.

In no-trump contracts you count your certain tricks and plan where to make the others needed. In trumps it is common to count losers, but it is helpful also to count your winners when they are obvious. That can point you on the right path.

1.   Dealer East : North-South vulnerable

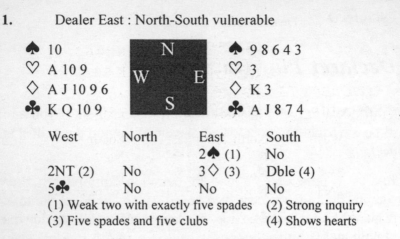

♠ 10
♥ A 10 9
♦ A J 10 9 6
♣ K Q 10 9

♠ 9 8 6 4 3
♥ 3
♦ K 3
♣ A J 8 7 4

West	North	East	South
		2♠ (1)	No
2NT (2)	No	3♦ (3)	Dble (4)
5♣	No	No	No

(1) Weak two with exactly five spades   (2) Strong inquiry
(3) Five spades and five clubs   (4) Shows hearts

North leads the ♥2 (thirds and fifths), taken by the ♥A. West plays the ♣K, club to the ♣A and back to the ♣Q. North follows once and then discards the ♥4 and the ♦2.

How should West continue? (Solution on page 116)

2.   Dealer South : North-South vulnerable

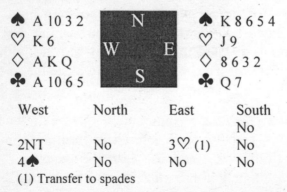

♠ A 10 3 2
♥ K 6
♦ A K Q
♣ A 10 6 5

♠ K 8 6 5 4
♥ J 9
♦ 8 6 3 2
♣ Q 7

West	North	East	South
			No
2NT	No	3♥ (1)	No
4♠	No	No	No

(1) Transfer to spades

Lead: ♦5 (thirds and fifths): two – ten – ace. All follow low on the ♠2 to the king. On the next spade, South discards the ♥8 (no interest in hearts) and you take the ♠A, North playing the ♠J.

How would you continue as West? (Solution on page 117)

3.   Dealer North : Love all

```
    ♠ 9              N              ♠ A K 10 6 5
    ♡ Q 10 4     W       E         ♡ A K 6 3
    ◇ Q J 10 9 7 3                 ◇ 2
    ♣ A 10 9         S             ♣ Q 7 2
```

West	North	East	South
	No	1♠	No
2◇	No	2♡	No
2NT	No	3NT	All pass

North leads the ♣6 (top of doubleton, middle-up-down or fourth-highest).

Which card do you play from dummy? Plan the play for West.
(Solution on page 118)

4.   Dealer North : North-South vulnerable

```
    ♠ A K J 10 9 7    N           ♠ 5 2
    ♡ 2           W       E       ♡ A K 10 9 4 3
    ◇ A 7 6 2                     ◇ K 3
    ♣ 7 3             S           ♣ A K 8
```

West	North	East	South
	No	1♡	No
1♠	No	3♡	No
3♠ (1)	No	4♠	No
4NT	No	5♡ (2)	No
6♠	No	No	No

(1) Forcing
(2) Two key cards for spades, no ♠Q

Lead: ♣2 (fourth-highest).

Plan the play. (When you come to draw trumps, North turns up with ♠Q 8 6 3. *(Solution on page 119)*

1.   Dealer East : North-South vulnerable

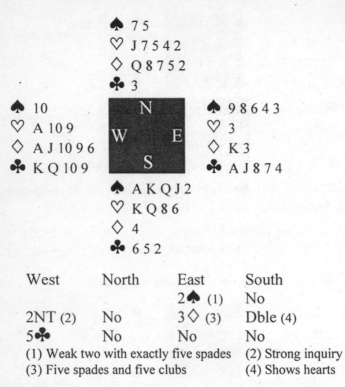

♠ 7 5
♡ J 7 5 4 2
♢ Q 8 7 5 2
♣ 3

♠ 10
♡ A 10 9
♢ A J 10 9 6
♣ K Q 10 9

♠ 9 8 6 4 3
♡ 3
♢ K 3
♣ A J 8 7 4

♠ A K Q J 2
♡ K Q 8 6
♢ 4
♣ 6 5 2

West	North	East	South
		2♠ (1)	No
2NT (2)	No	3♢ (3)	Dble (4)
5♣	No	No	No

(1) Weak two with exactly five spades   (2) Strong inquiry
(3) Five spades and five clubs   (4) Shows hearts

Source: Teams match on Bridge Base Online in 2005. North led the ♡2, taken by the ♡A. West played the ♣K, ♣9 to the ♣A and ♣7 to the ♣Q. North discarded the ♡4 and the ♢2. The rest of the play should be trivial: ♢K, diamond to the ace and ruff out the ♢Q. You lose just two spades.

The big danger is carelessness. You must be focussed all the time. West played the ♢J at trick 5 and let it run. He could have survived with ♢A next, but not after a diamond to the king. South won the spade exit and played another top spade, ruffed. Now West could not enjoy the diamond length.

2.   Dealer South : North-South vulnerable

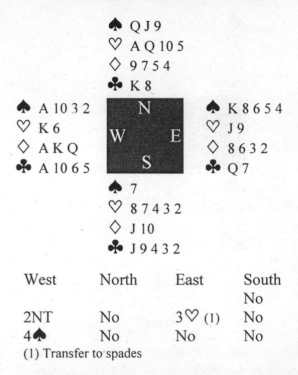

```
                    ♠ Q J 9
                    ♡ A Q 10 5
                    ◇ 9 7 5 4
                    ♣ K 8
  ♠ A 10 3 2                          ♠ K 8 6 5 4
  ♡ K 6             N                 ♡ J 9
  ◇ A K Q        W     E              ◇ 8 6 3 2
  ♣ A 10 6 5        S                 ♣ Q 7
                    ♠ 7
                    ♡ 8 7 4 3 2
                    ◇ J 10
                    ♣ J 9 4 3 2
```

West	North	East	South
			No
2NT	No	3♡ (1)	No
4♠	No	No	No

(1) Transfer to spades

Source: 2005 World Championships, Round 11. In one match both teams played in 4♠ by West. Both Norths led a diamond to the ten and ace and both declarers played a spade to the king and a spade to the ace. One West then cashed the ◇K, ◇Q before leading a low club. North rose with the ♣K, cashed the ♠Q and played the ◇9. West ruffed and had no entry to the clubs. The other declarer played a low club before cashing all the diamonds. Now there was an entry to reach the ♣A for a heart discard from dummy.

4♠ was played at 64 of 66 tables, 61 times on a diamond lead. Of these 61, 22 declarers made 4♠ and 39 failed.

3.   Dealer North : Love all

```
                    ♠ J 4 3 2
                    ♡ J 8 7
                    ◇ A K 8
                    ♣ 8 6 4
  ♠ 9                    N                ♠ A K 10 6 5
  ♡ Q 10 4                                ♡ A K 6 3
  ◇ Q J 10 9 7 3   W         E            ◇ 2
  ♣ A 10 9              S                 ♣ Q 7 2
                    ♠ Q 8 7
                    ♡ 9 5 2
                    ◇ 6 5 4
                    ♣ K J 5 3
```

West	North	East	South
	No	1♠	No
2◇	No	2♡	No
2NT	No	3NT	All pass

Source: Quarter-finals 2005 Bermuda Bowl and Venice Cup,
Board 65. All but two declarers in 3NT succeeded. At those
two tables North led a club: two – jack – ace. The ◇Q was
taken by the king and back came another club. One declarer
played low from dummy. South won with the ♣K and
played a third club. At the other declarer played dummy's
♣Q, but South ducked. In each case West now lacked the
entries to set up and enjoy the diamonds. Both tried a heart to
the ten, which lost and that was two down.

The solution is to play the ♣Q from dummy at trick one.
Whether the ♣Q wins or whether South's ♣K is taken by
the ace, West has an extra entry to hand via the club suit and
so can use the diamonds.

4. Dealer North : North-South vulnerable

<pre>
                    ♠ Q 8 6 3
                    ♡ 7 6 5
                    ◇ 10 5
                    ♣ J 10 4 2
  ♠ A K J 10 9 7   ┌───────┐   ♠ 5 2
  ♡ 2   │   N   │   ♡ A K 10 9 4 3
  ◇ A 7 6 2   │ W   E │   ◇ K 3
  ♣ 7 3   │   S   │   ♣ A K 8
                    └───────┘
                    ♠ 4
                    ♡ Q J 8
                    ◇ Q J 9 8 4
                    ♣ Q 9 6 5
</pre>

West	North	East	South
	No	1♡	No
1♠	No	3♡	No
3♠ (1)	No	4♠	No
4NT	No	5♡ (2)	No
6♠	No	No	No

(1) Forcing
(2) Two key cards for spades, no ♠Q

Source: 2006 National Teams Championships. 6♠ is an excellent slam, but was reached by only one third of the field. Many, too many, of those in 6♠ went down after a club lead when they tried to ruff the third round of diamonds in dummy.

There is a much better line. Take the club in dummy and play ♠A, ♠K, a heart to the ace and ruff a low heart. After the ♠J to North's ♠Q, win North's minor suit exit in dummy, ruff another low heart with a high trump and draw North's last trump. Dummy has a minor suit entry to reach the high hearts.

5.   Dealer East : Love all

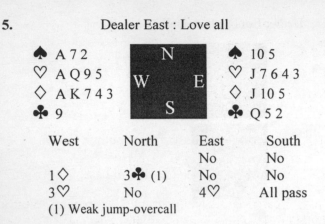

♠ A 7 2
♡ A Q 9 5
♢ A K 7 4 3
♣ 9

♠ 10 5
♡ J 7 6 4 3
♢ J 10 5
♣ Q 5 2

West	North	East	South
		No	No
1♢	3♣ (1)	No	No
3♡	No	4♡	All pass

(1) Weak jump-overcall

North leads the ♠6: five – queen – ace. West returns a spade and North wins with the ♠J. North switches to the ♣A, followed by the ♣J. West plays low in dummy, South also plays low and the ♣J is ruffed. West ruffs the third spade in dummy, both opponents following low.

How should West continue? (Solution on page 122)

6.   Dealer East : Love all

♠ K 7 5 4 2
♡ A 5
♢ A 10 3
♣ 10 5 4

♠ A 10 8
♡ J 10
♢ K 6 5
♣ K Q J 3 2

West	North	East	South
		1♣	No
1♠	No	2♣ (1)	No
2NT	No	3NT	All pass

(1) Dictated by system

North leads the ♢Q.

Playing pairs, how would you plan the play as West?
                    (Solution on page 123)

7.   Dealer South : Game all

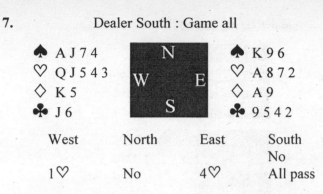

♠ A J 7 4
♡ Q J 5 4 3
◇ K 5
♣ J 6

♠ K 9 6
♡ A 8 7 2
◇ A 9
♣ 9 5 4 2

West	North	East	South
			No
1♡	No	4♡	All pass

East-West play 5-card majors and a strong 1♣ opening. West's opening is limited to 15 points, which explains East's 4♡.

North started with the ♣A, ♣K and continues with the ♣8 to South's ♣Q, which you ruff. The ♣10 is still out.

How would you plan the play from here?

(Solution on page 124)

8.   Dealer South : North-South vulnerable

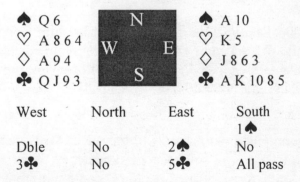

♠ Q 6
♡ A 8 6 4
◇ A 9 4
♣ Q J 9 3

♠ A 10
♡ K 5
◇ J 8 6 3
♣ A K 10 8 5

West	North	East	South
			1♠
Dble	No	2♠	No
3♣	No	5♣	All pass

North leads the ♠8.
Plan the play.
When you come to draw trumps, North turns up with ♣7-4-2.

(Solution on page 125)

5.   Dealer East : Love all

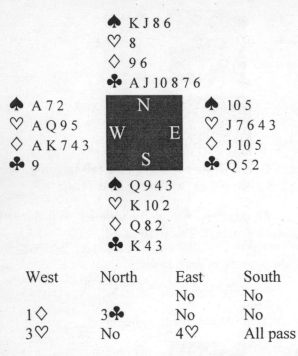

♠ K J 8 6
♥ 8
♦ 9 6
♣ A J 10 8 7 6

♠ A 7 2
♥ A Q 9 5
♦ A K 7 4 3
♣ 9

♠ 10 5
♥ J 7 6 4 3
♦ J 10 5
♣ Q 5 2

♠ Q 9 4 3
♥ K 10 2
♦ Q 8 2
♣ K 4 3

West	North	East	South
		No	No
1♦	3♣	No	No
3♥	No	4♥	All pass

Source: 2006 Pacific Asia Teams Championship, Round 6.
North led the ♠6, taken by the ace. Declarer returned a spade.
North won and switched to the ♣A, followed by the ♣J.
West ruffed the club and ruffed the third spade in dummy. What
should West do now ?

Declarer continued with a heart to the queen. This works if
South began with ♥K singleton or doubleton. When South
turned up with three hearts, declarer could not return to
dummy for the diamond finesse. The solution is easy enough.
When in dummy, play the ♦J. If it wins or is covered, you
switch to hearts. If the ♦J loses to North, you hope to reach
dummy with the ♦10 in order to play for no heart loser.

6. Dealer East : Love all

```
              ♠ Q J
              ♡ K 9 8
              ◇ Q J 9 4
              ♣ A 8 7 6
♠ K 7 5 4 2        N         ♠ A 10 8
♡ A 5                        ♡ J 10
◇ A 10 3       W      E      ◇ K 6 5
♣ 10 5 4          S          ♣ K Q J 3 2
              ♠ 9 6 3
              ♡ Q 7 6 4 3 2
              ◇ 8 7 2
              ♣ 9
```

West	North	East	South
		1♣	No
1♠	No	2♣ (1)	No
2NT	No	3NT	All pass

(1) Dictated by system

Source: 2007 National Pairs Championship. North leads the ◇Q and you note that you have missed a much better spot in 4♠ (East might have bid 3♠ over 2NT). You also see the danger if they find the heart switch when they come in with the ♣A. To make a diamond continuation attractive, you take the ◇K in dummy and drop the ◇10 from hand.

North takes the ♣A on the third round and continues with a diamond despite South's signal for a switch to hearts. You win with the ◇A and cross to the ♠A to cash the rest of the clubs. Later you can pick up all the spades and make twelve tricks for a shared top.

7.   Dealer South : Game all

```
                        ♠ Q 8
                        ♡ 10 9
                        ◇ Q 10 8 7 2
                        ♣ A K 10 8
    ♠ A J 7 4         ┌─────────┐      ♠ K 9 6
    ♡ Q J 5 4 3       │    N    │      ♡ A 8 7 2
    ◇ K 5             │ W     E │      ◇ A 9
    ♣ J 6             │    S    │      ♣ 9 5 4 2
                      └─────────┘
                        ♠ 10 5 3 2
                        ♡ K 6
                        ◇ J 6 4 3
                        ♣ Q 7 3
```

West	North	East	South
			No
1♡	No	4♡	All pass

Source: 2007 Yeh Bros Cup. North began with the ♣A, ♣K and the ♣8 to the queen, ruffed by West. With both the ♠J finesse, the normal play in spades, and the heart finesse failing, you might expect 4♡ to be one off. A different approach has much to commend it, especially if South has signalled an odd number of clubs. Play a low heart to the ♡A, followed by the ◇K and a diamond to the ◇A. Then play dummy's fourth club and ruff it. Now exit with the ♡Q.

If down to ♡K bare, North must play a spade or concede a ruff-and-discard. If South is left with ♡K only and exits with a spade, play low from hand. This succeeds if South began with the ♠Q or the ♠10. If hearts are 3-1, you can take the spade finesse later.

8. Dealer South : North-South vulnerable

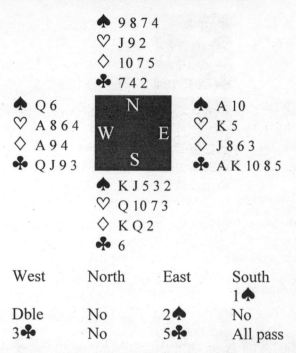

♠ 9 8 7 4
♡ J 9 2
◇ 10 7 5
♣ 7 4 2

♠ Q 6
♡ A 8 6 4
◇ A 9 4
♣ Q J 9 3

♠ A 10
♡ K 5
◇ J 8 6 3
♣ A K 10 8 5

♠ K J 5 3 2
♡ Q 10 7 3
◇ K Q 2
♣ 6

West	North	East	South
			1♠
Dble	No	2♠	No
3♣	No	5♣	All pass

Source: Finals of a 2007 Zonal Teams Championship. At one table East bid 3NT over 3♣ and that was no problem. At the other three tables West played in 5♣ after similar auctions to the one given. North led a spade, taken by the ♠A.

One West played off three rounds of trumps, ♡K, ♡A, heart ruff, spade exit. When South could exit with the ♡Q, West had to lose two diamonds for one down. The other two declarers did better. They played ♠A, ♣A, ♡K, followed by a heart to the ♡A. Next came a heart ruff, club to hand, heart ruff. Leaving the last trump out, they exited with the ♠Q. South won, but was endplayed. As South is marked with the points, West just plays low from hand on South's ◇K exit.

9.   Dealer East : North-South vulnerable

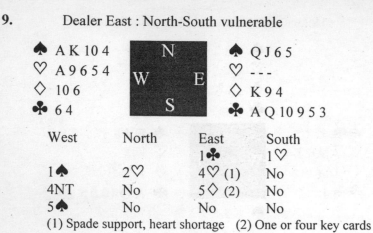

♠ A K 10 4	♠ Q J 6 5
♡ A 9 6 5 4	♡ - - -
◊ 10 6	◊ K 9 4
♣ 6 4	♣ A Q 10 9 5 3

West	North	East	South
		1♣	1♡
1♠	2♡	4♡ (1)	No
4NT	No	5◊ (2)	No
5♠	No	No	No

(1) Spade support, heart shortage   (2) One or four key cards

North leads the ♡Q. *Plan the play.* Suppose you take the ♡A and finesse in clubs, losing. Back comes a heart, ruffed in dummy. *How should you continue? (Solution on page 127)*

10.   Dealer East : North-South vulnerable

♠ - - -	♠ 5 3 2
♡ J 10 7 5 2	♡ 6
◊ J 10 8 6	◊ A K Q 7
♣ A K Q 9	♣ 8 7 5 4 2

West	North	East	South
		No	1♣ (1)
1♡	1♠	Dble (2)	Rdble (3)
4◊	4♠	5◊	Dble
No	No	No	

(1) 3+ clubs   (2) For takeout   (3) Support double, three spades

North leads the ♣J, South following with the ♣3. North-South play 5-card majors. What is South's exact shape? Suppose you play ◊6: three – ace – two and ruff a spade. You continue with the ◊10: nine – king – four and ruff another spade. *What next?*

(Solution on page 128)

9.   Dealer East : North-South vulnerable

```
              ♠ 9 3 2
              ♡ Q J 10
              ◇ J 7 5 3
              ♣ K 8 7
♠ A K 10 4      N        ♠ Q J 6 5
♡ A 9 6 5 4              ♡ - - -
◇ 10 6       W     E     ◇ K 9 4
♣ 6 4           S        ♣ A Q 10 9 5 3
              ♠ 8 7
              ♡ K 8 7 3 2
              ◇ A Q 8 2
              ♣ J 2
```

West	North	East	South
		1♣	1♡
1♠	2♡	4♡ (1)	No
4NT	No	5◇ (2)	No
5♠	No	No	No

(1) Spade support, heart shortage
(2) One or four key cards

Source: Final of a 2007 National Teams Championship. At one table East-West had a free run to 4♠. Declarer won the trump lead with the ace, played a club to the queen and had no trouble after that. At the other table West was in 5♠ on the ♡Q lead, taken by the ace, and played a club to the ten.

South won and returned a heart, ruffed in dummy. Declarer now needs to come to hand with a trump and take another club finesse. When that wins, draw trumps and claim. In practice West continued with the ♣A and a club ruff. When a diamond to the king lost, the contract failed.

10.   Dealer East : North-South vulnerable

                ♠ K Q J 10 9 8 6
                ♡ 9 8 3
                ♢ 9 3
                ♣ J

♠ - - -	**N**	♠ 5 3 2
♡ J 10 7 5 2	**W** **E**	♡ 6
♢ J 10 8 6		♢ A K Q 7
♣ A K Q 9	**S**	♣ 8 7 5 4 2

                ♠ A 7 4
                ♡ A K Q 4
                ♢ 5 4 2
                ♣ 10 6 3

West	North	East	South
		No	1♣ (1)
1♡	1♠	Dble (2)	Rdble (3)
4♢	4♠	5♢	Dble
No	No	No	

(1) 3+ clubs (2) For takeout (3) Support double, three spades

Source: Final, National Open Teams Selection. Declarer took the ♣J lead with the ace, played a diamond to the ace and led the ♡6. South took the ♡Q and gave North a club ruff. There was no way any more for declarer to succeed.

The bidding and lead marks South with exactly three clubs and three spades. As South would open 1♢ with four diamonds, South's pattern has to be 3-4-3-3. West can take the ♣A, play a diamond to the ace, ruff a spade, cross to the ♢K and ruff a spade. With North out of diamonds and the ♢9 falling, cash the ♣K, ♣Q and exit with a heart. They can have a spade, but you ruff the next major suit card and draw the last trump, on which you play the ♣9 to unblock the clubs. Very neat.